Spiritual Growth and Personal Development

RAISING YOUR VIBE
The Guide for Becoming a Lightworker

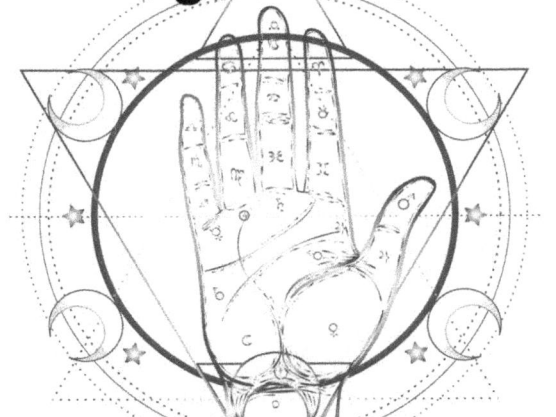

MONIQUE JOINER SIEDLAK

Oshun Publications

Raising Your Vibe: The Guide for Becoming a Lightworker © Copyright 2021 by Monique Joiner Siedlak
ISBN: 978-1-950378-98-2
All rights reserved

The content contained within this book may not be reproduced, duplicated or transmitted without direct written permission from the author or the publisher.

Under no circumstances will any blame or legal responsibility be held against the publisher, or author, for any damages, reparation, or monetary loss due to the information contained within this book, either directly or indirectly.

Legal Notice

This book is copyright protected. It is only for personal use. You cannot amend, distribute, sell, use, quote or paraphrase any part, or the content within this book, without the consent of the author or publisher.

Disclaimer Notice

Please note the information contained within this document is for educational and entertainment purposes only. All effort has been executed to present accurate, up to date, reliable, complete information. No warranties of any kind are declared or implied. Readers acknowledge that the author is not engaged in the rendering of legal, financial, medical or professional advice. The content within this book has been derived from various sources. Please consult a licensed professional before attempting any techniques outlined in this book.

By reading this document, the reader agrees that under no circumstances is the author responsible for any losses, direct or indirect, that are incurred as a result of the use of the information contained within this document, including, but not limited to, errors, omissions, or inaccuracies.

Cover Design by MJS
Cover Image by
Published by Oshun Publications
www.oshunpublications.com

More Books in the Series

Spiritual Growth and Personal Development
Creative Visualization
Astral Projection for Beginners
Meditation for Beginners
Reiki for Beginners
Manifesting With the Law of Attraction
Being an Empath Today
Healing Your Inner Child: A Guide into Shadow Work

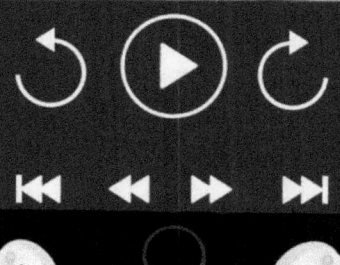

WANT UPDATES, FREEBIES & GIVEAWAYS?!

YOGA FOR DEPRESSION

MONIQUE JOINER SIEDLAK

JOIN MY NEWSLETTER!

mojosiedlak.com/self-help-and-yoga-newsletter

Contents

Introduction	xiii
1. What Is a Lightworker?	1
2. What Does a Lightworker Do?	13
3. Types of Lightworkers	21
4. The Four Pillars of Lightworkers	37
5. Seven Signs You May Be a Lightworker	41
6. Self Care For the Lightworker	51
7. Meditation as a Lightworker	71
8. Lightworker Syndrome	77
Conclusion	83
References	85
About the Author	89
Other Books by the Author	91
Last Chance	95
Thank You!	97

Introduction

"Your essence is fabricated from the stardust lace and earthly soil. As you wander, you call in your soul closer until one day you embody it." —Sylvia Salow

We live in a world where the polarity of good and evil is known and acknowledged. We all say that we want to do what is good and right, yet our planet is currently overflowing with chaos and darkness. How is this possible?

For most people, when they say they are committed to doing what is good, the fact is that they are only committed to doing what is beneficial or not harmful to themselves. The moment that goodness does not benefit them or harms them in any way, they are hesitant to do it. We all want to make the world a lighter and better place, but not everyone can do so in a meaningful way. Lightworkers are souls whose life mission is to be a conduit of light into the world. Some do this through transmuting darkness, healing the world, and others through teaching. Some people bring light into the world by inspiring us to embrace our authentic selves. Others do it by helping others as they ascend closer to unity with the universe and Source. Being a lightworker is a special calling that originates from realms beyond this one.

Introduction

I need to explain some foundational ideas and concepts before I can begin unpacking who lightworkers are and explaining their purpose. I will briefly explain what I mean by the higher self, the soul, the spirit, the ego, and the shadow. I will discuss these concepts and many others in detail as the book progresses.

When we speak of the spirit, we speak of God/Source's consciousness. It embodies all that is in existence. It is the essence of all that is alive, meaning that everything that ever has and ever will exist is only made possible through the Source's consciousness. The spirit consists of matter and energy. The spirit is a part of the Source, but it is not Source. Source transcends matter and energy, being more than we could ever perceive or comprehend. The spirit is what connects us to the Source. In this book, I will be using the words "spirit" and "universe" interchangeably to mean the same thing: The consciousness of the Source. The soul is our eternal consciousness, and it comes from the spirit. Many spiritual teachings and ascended masters say that the soul is merely pieces of the spirit fragmented during the Big Bang. Although we are all products of the spirit, our soul is what gives us our own spiritual identity. It is our highest self that is connected both to the spirit and to other souls. The soul is unchanged and can reincarnate into different beings in different worlds at different times.

When our souls reincarnate into the physical, it does so in a state of amnesia or sleep. Our inner self then fragments into two parts, the ego, and the shadow. The ego is the conscious part of ourselves that allows us to be self-aware. It is the part of ourselves that can think and process sensory stimuli, allowing us to experience life. It is driven by the desire for security, understanding, and acceptance. So, it defines itself by worldly gain and labels so that our physical beings can assimilate and be part of society. Society provides us with security and the fulfillment of our needs. Because our ego is driven by

Introduction

the need for security and acceptance, it builds our physical sense of identity only on the attributes which are deemed socially acceptable or advantageous. The ego makes this distinction through our experiences with others. As we interact with other people, the ego notes which of our attributes are socially acceptable and necessary for our survival and which are shunned and make it difficult for us to assimilate into society. The ego will not want to identify with those attributes of our soul that are not socially acceptable and will repress them into our unconscious mind, known as the shadow. In this way, our soul is both conscious and unconscious.

The ego is only a part of the self (the soul). When you begin your journey to spiritual awakening, you are forced to confront your shadow. Begin to unify it with your ego because the spirit only recognizes and communicates with your soul. As you remember, when you are reincarnated into the physical world, your soul is fragmented into the ego and the soul. Your spiritual awakening requires you to do shadow work so that your shadow can be brought into consciousness. When you begin to ascend, your ego' dies'—that is to say, it relinquishes control of your consciousness. It becomes unified with the shadow, thus awakening your soul. Your soul is your highest, eternal and spiritual self. As your connection to your higher self-strengthens, you can transcend the physical world's limitations, and you adopt a higher perspective, one that is aligned with the spirit. In this space of higher consciousness, we realize that our ego-mind idea of the self is entirely warped and false. The ego-self sees itself as different from others and competes against them for survival, love, and acceptance. When we are connected to the spirit, we understand that we are connected to each other and to the Source, although we are all individuals. There is no need to compete for survival, and we don't need to be or do anything outside of our authentic selves to be loved and accepted.

However, because we are still grounded in the physical

Introduction

world, we struggle to ultimately unify the ego and the shadow. We become distracted by the chaos and noise of this realm and lose the connection to our highest self. It's important to remember that the ego functions to protect us from harm and uncertainty. Whenever we are faced with new or unforeseen circumstances, our ego kicks in and takes control of our consciousness. This breaks our link to the spirit and its higher consciousness. This is why we say that spiritual awakening is a journey that requires intentionality and consistency. You must constantly decide to rise above your ego-mind and adopt a higher, spiritual perspective.

This book provides a systematic outline of everything you need to know about the life and journey of a lightworker. It begins with demonstrating to you precisely what a lightworker is so that you can understand their purpose in this world. You will get to know how a lightworker goes from living an average life to undergoing a spiritual awakening. You will come to understand what 'dark night of the soul' is and why all lightworkers have to experience it before they can experience ascension. The book also explains shadow work and how it is crucial to the awakening journey. Finally, the first chapter concludes with a thorough explanation of what ascension is and how to know if you have ascended to the next level of consciousness.

You will also learn how lightworkers can go about their daily lives living as consciously spiritual beings grounded in a physical realm. I will provide examples of ways that a lightworker can practically make money while living a purpose-driven life. These include various careers as mindfulness practitioners, healers, scientists, and activists.

The book teaches you a simple, basic understanding of the five different dimensions relevant to a lightworker's gifts and talents. It then moves to define the various kinds of lightworkers on earth and their role in raising the collective consciousness, and which traits they possess. You will also learn of the four pillars of commonality between the works of all lightworkers.

After learning what lightworkers do, how their purposes differ, and how they can make a living while on earth, you will learn about the signs of a lightworker so that you can identify if you are one as well. This chapter looks at the familiar markers of each lightworker's life and explains why they all resonate with specific characteristics. It highlights the importance of acknowledging your purpose and living a life that honors your role as a bringer of love and light into the world.

By this point in the book, you will be aware of some of the pitfalls and difficulties of being a lightworker. You will learn here about the mental, physical, emotional, and spiritual wellness of a lightworker and how to take care of each of these spheres. You will know how to do various practices and techniques that will unblock your energy field. Align your chakras to ensure a continuous energy flow in your body, grounding techniques to balance your spiritual and physical awareness, and how to connect with your intuition. You will also learn how to find peace and joy in everyday life, manage your emotional reactivity to unforeseen circumstances and overcome your emotional triggers. Lastly, you will learn how to overcome the fears that come from trying to live a purpose-driven life with the realities of providing for yourself in this world. This final chapter includes a helpful explanation of how to step into your power as a lightworker and start walking in the universe's abundance.

This book will teach the difference between a person who does deeds and a soul whose life purpose is to radiate light and love into the earth.

By the end of this book, you will have all the information you need to determine if you are a lightworker and how to activate your calling at your disposal. Unlike most people on this earth, you will make an informed decision and walk into your destiny knowing much more than most. This book contains precious wisdom that should not be squandered once attained. What you are about to read may just change the course of your life forever. And if you take what you learn here and apply it to your life, you may just change the course of mankind's path as well.

ONE

What Is a Lightworker?

"As far as we can discern, the sole purpose of human existence is to kindle a light in the darkness of mere being." -Carl Jung

There are many things that scientists and spiritualists vehemently disagree about. Still, one of the things they agree on is this: All matter is made up of energy that vibrates at varying frequencies. Those who are spiritually inclined understand that this energy is the spiritual realm, affecting our emotional, physical, and mental states. We know that lower (dark) frequencies are attracted by negative/dense thoughts and emotions, which block your energy fields and drain you of light energy. These include fear, shame, anger, anxiety, and jealousy.

On the other hand, higher (light) frequencies are attracted by positive/light thoughts and emotions that uplift and invigorate you. These include love, compassion. Joy, confidence, and peace.

The concept of intentionally raising your frequency has become popularized in western culture through spiritual practices, such as meditation and yoga, which promote mindfulness. When you raise your frequency, you focus on your thoughts, emotions, and environment. You become aware of the frequency at which both you and your environment are vibrating. This awareness is known as consciousness. The higher you vibrate, the higher your state of consciousness. While mindful practices primarily focus on the self and raising individual consciousness, light working focuses on harnessing light energy. Sharing it with others, therefore increasing the collective consciousness. To raise the collective consciousness is to raise the consciousness of other souls, plants, animals. And the planet itself.

As the name suggests, lightworkers are souls whose purpose is to do the work of radiating light energy into the world and raising the collective consciousness. They are called to be in service of mankind and to help earth ascend into the next dimension. Some are called to help, heal and encourage other souls to awaken and begin their ascension towards unity in the spiritual realm. Others are called to guide the awakened souls during their ascension. We will detail the different dimensions and how lightworkers go about fulfilling their purpose in chapter 3. For now, it suffices to say that while all lightworkers are called to bring light into the world, the gifts, skills, and techniques they use towards this goal are varied. Lightworkers have an innate understanding of the connectedness of all things (people, animals, plants, and the universe) and have a deep desire to serve the greater good. Lightworkers can be found in all pockets of society and are not bound to specific places or social spheres. Their only commonality is that everything they do is driven by love, compassion, and kindness.

Unconditional love lies at the core of a lightworker's purpose because it is the foundation of the spirit and Source. Lightworkers do their work in service to both. It requires a complete understanding and acceptance of all beings, their shortcomings, repressed emotions, fears, and hidden bad habits. There is no shame, fear, or any other dense emotion or thought involved in unconditional love because it is not transactional. Transactional love is conditional and relies on the idea that there is a scarcity of love in the universe. It peddles the belief that for you to receive love, you must trade something in return. The moment you stop fulfilling the conditions of this love, it is revoked.

In contrast, unconditional love is given freely without the need for any transactions. You do not need to do anything to get it, nor is your access to it limited by anything. Unconditional love requires nothing more than for you to be your authentic self, as this alone makes you worthy of being loved. This kind of love lies at the heart of all souls and is awakened as we undergo our spiritual awakening. When you give and receive unconditional love, all aspects of your life improve because you can embrace your highest self. You see and understand all the parts that make you unique without any judgment. This embrace allows you to coax your inner darkness into the light and to bring both into harmony with one another. It's then easy for you to raise your consciousness and connect to the spirit and Source.

When your soul is reincarnated into the physical world, it is asleep. All souls need to undergo a spiritual awakening where they are reconnected with their higher selves and come to unlock the universal truth of our interconnectedness. This is especially true for lightworkers who need to awaken to their purpose in service to mankind. For a select few, this awakening happens during their youth, while they are still trying to understand the ways of this world and how they can relate to it. They come to know their purpose early on in life and start living a life aligned with it. Unfortunately, this is not the case for most people. For the majority, your soul fragments into the ego and the shadow, and your ego take charge of your conscious mind, leaving the shadow rejected and untouched. In such cases, you are prone to live a life of traumatic and isolating experiences meant to push you towards spiritual awakening. When people experience trauma or are isolated from their communities, they tend to draw further into themselves as a defense mechanism against future hurt. During this time, they find themselves analyzing their personalities, their life choices, and how they interact with others. This is when they will confront their shadows and begin experiencing a spiritual awakening.

Unfortunately, these traumatic/isolating experiences do not always have the desired effect. Instead of making people introspect and realizing their authentic and highest self, these experiences sometimes cause people to completely shut the world out in anger. Instead of recognizing and engaging in their purpose as lightworkers, these people will go through life spiritually asleep. Preferring to protect themselves rather than risking being dejected and in pain again. These experiences may even leave them bitter and unwilling to help others in any capacity. This stops them from confronting their inner darkness and venturing on the journey towards spiritual awareness and connection with the universe. Many lightworkers have been lost this way, preferring a life of physical numbness to the sensitivity of being a lightworker.

If you are a lightworker, your spiritual awakening will require you to confront your internal darkness. Learn to love yourself entirely before connecting to your higher self and learning how to effectively channel your inner light. This process of self-realization is often triggered by the incidents that shake you out of your conditioned rhythm, forcing you to stop and take stock of your lives. Perhaps you are suddenly faced with a large, unprecedented, and unexpected stumbling block in your career, and you have no idea how you are meant to overcome it. Or you may have suddenly lost someone close to you, perhaps a partner, a friend, or a parent. This person could have been the foundation upon which your support system was built. Now it feels as though the ground has been viciously pulled from under you, with no warning whatsoever. Sometimes the triggering event does not happen to you but to those in your community, making you realize that you have been living under a false illusion.

Perhaps you live in a neighborhood that you consider to be relatively safe. So you've never thought much of crime in the area as there seemingly is none. Then one day, you hear that there was a burglary at the house right across from yours. This unsettles you, so you speak with your neighbors on how you can make your neighborhood safer, only to find out that there have been quite a few break-ins in the past two years! Now, it seems as if the rise in criminal activity has been a hot topic for some time now, but you were blissfully unaware, and you ask yourself how you could have missed this. You immerse yourself in reading up on crime statistics, and the more you read, the more unsafe you feel the world is, not only for yourself and your family but the world over. Something like this may send you spinning headfirst into an existential dread of hopelessness and fear.

There are countless ways in which you might suddenly find yourself at a complete loss, where you may feel like your entire worldview has come crashing down. You are left flailing about in an ocean of depression and despair, barely able to keep your head above the water. This period of overwhelming despair is known as the "dark night of the soul." When lightworkers undergo intense shadow work, they attempt to raise their consciousness and move closer towards enlightenment.

The Dark Night of the Soul and Ascension

The phrase "dark night of the soul" comes from a poem called La noche oscura del alma, written by 16th-century poet and mystic John of the Cross. In the poem, he laments the problematic experience of moving towards being in union with God (Source). When experiencing a dark night of the soul, lightworkers often find themselves overcome by despondence, anxiety, fear, and other dense emotions. They feel rudderless and utterly disconnected from Source. They no longer find motivation in the things that once sparked joy within them. This spiritual crisis leads the lightworker to question the divine order and timing of the universe. Suddenly, nothing is enjoyable and social niceties become burdensome. The lightworkers will isolate themselves more than usual. Spend time immersing themselves deeper into philosophy and spiritual practices in an attempt to gain new and deeper understandings of life and recenter themselves.

During this time of reflection, lightworkers begin to question their thoughts, views, and beliefs. They pull at every part of themselves, hoping to reassemble themselves in a way that will make life make sense again. By doing this, they begin to confront their shadow and start the journey towards discovering and embracing their authentic selves. The more they do shadow work, the higher they ascend through the various levels of spiritual awakening. The more light they can radiate onto others and into the world in general.

The term "shadow work" was popularized by celebrated analytical psychologist Carl Jung when he introduced the idea that our sense of self consists of the ego and the shadow. According to Jungian psychology, our shadow consists of dark emotions. Thoughts and habits that our conscious egos do not want to associate with, such as jealousy, codependency, resentment, and anger. It also houses the habits and characteristics that we have been conditioned to hide and repress into our subconscious minds. Because they are considered undesirable in some way, such as excessive pride.

Engaging in shadow work requires you to objectively explore all of your emotions, trigger points, thoughts, and habits without judgment. This allows you to bring your shadow into the light (the conscious mind) and figure out how to create an internal environment where your subconscious lives in harmony and love with your conscious ego, thus reuniting your soul. This is important because until you reach enlightenment, your soul remains fragmented in the physical world. Because of this, you will continually oscillate between the different levels of ascension. Although you have become awakened, you will fail to fully comprehend the interconnected nature of all that is until you reach total enlightenment. No matter how high you vibrate, there will remain a part of you that feels separate from the universe. As such, you will always find yourself battling against dark energies and having to make a conscious effort to overcome them. The higher you ascend, the easier this becomes. However, it is still a struggle to be contended with until you reach the final level of spiritual awakening.

Shadow work lays the foundation that allows you to be fully connected with the spirit and Source. First, by repairing your soul and bringing you in connection with your highest self. Doing shadow work helps lightworkers vibrate higher, increasing their capacity to absorb and radiate light to others and the world at large. It also helps them fulfill their purpose with compassion and form genuine connections because of their personal experiences with trauma, rejection, and the hardships associated with a spiritual awakening. It allows them to have genuine compassion and understanding for others undergoing the same thing. They know how easy it is to feel overcome by the darkness. To lose the budding connection they had with their higher selves and struggle with being both awakened and physically grounded.

In the spiritual world, the experience of a soul during a spiritual awakening is called ascension. During this experience, our energies move from lower, darker frequencies to higher, lighter ones. This new lightness moves us closer to the Source. So we shed our old selves and our earthly perceptions as we adopt a higher perspective and become more aware of the connectedness of everything and everyone in the universe. The shift from a physical understanding of reality (where we see ourselves as separate from the world and each other) to a true and spiritual awareness (where we gain the knowledge that everything is connected and that our job is to raise the collective consciousness and bring other souls and our planet closer to the light) changes how we think, react and speak. We gain new universal wisdom and let go of our old, ignorant ways. Each level of ascension brings with it a different, higher perception.

Ascension does not detach you from your physical form because you need to remain grounded to this planet to execute your mission. The only exception is for souls who have reached total enlightenment and have ascended to the fifth dimension. These beings transcend the physical form and can inhabit a light body. However, some choose to remain in their physical form to guide others along their paths to total enlightenment. For the most part, ascension comes as moments, either short or continuous, where you experience a new level of consciousness and become privy to new and deeper understandings of how the universe works. The most important part of ascension is to awaken the lightworker to their core frequency. This frequency is what allows you to think and see things differently from others, even before you undergo a spiritual awakening. This frequency is usually within the dimension in which their spiritual gifts function. However, lightworkers need to experience all the different levels of ascension and don't just awaken at the level that allows them access to their spiritual gifts. Shadow work facilitates the initial awakening. When you confront and analyze your shadow, you come to understand why you never quite fit in, why your interests and opinions were often diametrically opposed to those of society. This understanding will, at some point, manifest in a change in personality, lifestyle, and behavior. You will shift from an earthly perspective of scarcity and competition to a spiritual perspective of abundance and love.

Psychospiritual teacher Mateo Sol writes of the five different forms of ascension that souls undergo. First, there is an awakening of the mind, which frees you from perceptions of the ego-mind in favor of knowledge from the spirit-mind. Your perspective of reality shifts to a higher frequency as you receive new wisdom on the workings of the spirit and how we relate to it. The awakening of the mind doesn't always follow any fundamental changes in how you think or carry yourself in the physical world. Mainly because what is revealed to you is so different from what you have realized as truth that you are prone to dismiss it. Even if you don't accept this new wisdom right away, you will continue to think on and investigate the integrity of these revelations. This happens because, as a lightworker, you always want to learn and gain a deeper understanding of life. Your ego-mind and spirit-mind will begin competing for dominance, so to speak. In the end, you will come to accept this new wisdom that has been revealed to you on how your world works with everything in the universe.

Second, there is an awakening of a new personality inspired by the revelations you gain from your mental awakening. Along with a perspective shift, you will feel inclined to delve deeper into your shadow so that you can rid yourself of all the views and beliefs that were constructed contrary to the universal truth. These may include limiting beliefs over money, your talents, and your place in the world. When you begin to dispel the warped notions you had, you come closer to accepting your authentic self and seeing the worth in being all you are. This births a new personality in the physical world. One that expresses the parts of yourself that were hidden in shame. This includes big things that have affected how you view yourself and small things like hobbies you had to abandon. Let's say that you used to enjoy singing but were shamed and told you have a terrible singing voice. When you embrace your authentic self again, you will continue singing regardless of what people say because it brings you joy and lights you up. Your consciousness increases in tandem with your authenticity. The more authentic you are, the stronger your connection to your higher self. As a result, you yearn to learn more about your spirituality because you feel lighter and happier than you have ever been, and you want more of that.

Third, you undergo an awakening of spiritual energy awakened to your personal access to the universe's energetic fields. This is a significant awakening for those who are called to be gatekeepers, dreamers, and seers. This awakening is triggered through physical, spiritual practices such as yoga and meditation because they align the mind with the body and the spirit. When this happens, you experience a heightened sense of connectedness to all beings and the universe itself. You become aware of the grid lines that connect all human hearts and the ley lines connecting earth with other astral planes and the universe itself. If you are a gatekeeper, you will realize why you always felt a strange energy in specific locations. These will be places where portals and gateways are located, where the universe's energy pours into the planet in a concentrated and continuous flow. These are usually places with ancient sacred sites of the Mayan, Egyptian, Incan, and other ancient civilizations that were aware of the electromagnetic field around the earth. They created sites to harness that energy and ground the planet.

Fourth, you can experience an awakening of the soul where you see glimpses of your highest, eternal self. These are moments where your soul experiences a total reunification of itself. These moments can be brief and spontaneous, or they can occur sporadically over a long period. They usually happen in moments of complete mindfulness, like during a meditation or a prayer. In these moments, you gain a deeper understanding of universal laws and become more compassionate and loving because you see that we are all the product of one spirit.

Finally, you can achieve a total awakening. This is known by most people as enlightenment. At this level, you are fully conscious of the unity of all beings to the universe and

Source, and you experience what Jungian psychology calls a complete ego death. Any sense of separation between yourself and others is obliterated, and you "feel like nothing and everything all at once." This doesn't mean that you lose your sense of self, merely the idea that you are intrinsically different and separate from others and the planet. You come to understand that although your soul is your individual consciousness, it's a product of and is connected to the spirit and Source. Enlightenment differs from the other types of ascension. It cannot be induced through any known spiritual teachings or practices. It only happens when the spirit deems you ready and able to have the earthy veil of reality completely removed from you.

It's important to note that being awakened to a certain level of truth does not necessarily mean that you will remain there indefinitely. You still have to fight your ego-mind into accepting whichever universal truth has been revealed to you. So, you will go back and forth between being connected to this higher perspective and abandoning it in favor of an earthly perspective. During this phase of your ascension, you are simply awakened to the truth but not yet settled in it. When you fully come to accept the knowledge and wisdom revealed to you, you constantly vibrate at this higher frequency. At this phase, you are enlightened to the understanding of that specific dimension. This is different from total enlightenment, where you experience ego death.

Once you begin your journey to spiritual awakening, each ascension level brings you a higher consciousness and brings you closer to possibly experiencing total enlightenment. Your life's purpose comes into sharper focus as you gravitate towards the things that will help you execute your mission. All levels of ascension lead to you shedding the perceptions of reality created by your ego-mind, including any limiting beliefs and destructive habits. You must confront the truth about yourself at every new level and reflect on who you definitely are. Question the things you once thought to be constant facts of life, and embrace a new way of being. During ascension, you experience a complete overhaul of self and are emptied of all the things your ego made you think were essential to your survival. This is a daunting journey, and you will often feel overwhelmed and begin to question your intuition and discoveries as you try to reconcile the limitlessness of your eternal being. Your ego functions to protect you from the dangers of the unknown, and ascension is the ultimate experience of the unknown, so it will fight you every step of the way. Instead of succumbing to your ego, you will have to decide to intentionally and consistently work on unifying your ego with your shadow. When you do this, you gain an increased capacity to carry and spread light.

Spiritual awakening is a lifelong journey that is to be savored. Each step brings you new wisdom that will enrich your earthly experience. As with most things in the spiritual world, it's essential to be patient with yourself through your awakening. Some days will be more challenging than others, and sometimes you'll want to curl up in a corner and disappear. Remember that with every change you experience, there will be a transitional period. All you need to do is choose to consistently walk the path. It helps to find yourself a community to help you through the tough times and share the triumphs. The universe will bring you the tools and people you will need along the way.

TWO

What Does a Lightworker Do?

"IN THE RIGHT LIGHT, AT THE RIGHT TIME, EVERYTHING IS extraordinary." -Aaron Rose

You now understand that a lightworker's mission on earth is to spread light, love, and hope. But how exactly do they do this? Well, there is a myriad of ways in which a lightworker can effectively execute their mission. This chapter deals with how lightworkers can fulfill their purpose in the physical world. They have guides who will inform them of the best way to align their earthly lives with their spiritual purpose.

Before we delve into how lightworkers live out their purpose on earth, it's important to understand how they can do this work. Lightworkers are only able to begin intentionally living out their purpose once their souls have been awakened. When their souls are awake, they can unleash the skills and spiritual gifts they are given in accordance with their purpose. The ego is a part of the soul that is awake and in control of the body's awareness. It has some of the soul's attributes. So lightworkers will have some sense of wanting to do work that benefits the greater good and is somehow connected to everyone. As such, lightworkers can still partially fulfill their purpose when their souls are not yet awakened, but they won't be able to do it as effectively. This is why they need to consciously tame their egos and their shadows so that the soul can be united and awakened. As they ascend higher and increase their capacity, lightworkers uncover more depth in their spiritual gifts and skills.

Once they have begun the journey of unifying the soul, lightworkers need to keep their energy field as light and open as possible. For this reason, they have a greater capacity to radiate love and light into the world. While they can channel their energy towards specific people, it is so strong and constant that their mere presence positively impacts those around them and raises the planet's consciousness.

What Do Lightworkers Do For A Living?

So, now onto a more physically practical matter: How do lightworkers make money? How can they pursue their purpose while making sure that they can pay their bills and feed themselves? We need to remember that although the universe will ensure that all their physical needs are met, it does not concern itself with feeding their ego. The universe understands that it's difficult for lightworkers to focus all their energy on fulfilling their spiritual purpose when they are worried about paying the bills. So it ensures that you will have your earthly needs met, but it is not concerned with your desire to afford a luxury vehicle. That is not to say that the universe wants you to live a mediocre and unfulfilling life. Still, as an awakened being, you understand that true fulfillment can only be found in unity with the spirit and Source, not in material objects. The universe will not allow you to manifest things that are not vibrating at the same frequency as your consciousness. Suppose your quest for wealth brings you out of alignment with the universe. In that case, you will have to abandon your purpose in pursuit of your undertaking. Because of this, it may be impossible to gain immense material wealth without jeopardizing the delicate balance between spiritual connectedness and physical groundedness.

Due to the nature of their purpose, lightworkers generally work in fields that contribute to the greater good of humanity where they can heal, encourage, guide, and teach others. Lightworkers that are called to heal often do so with some form of physical touch. They can work as doctors and nurses, healing people with touch and conventional/Western medicine. Some can work as licensed massage therapists or reiki practitioners. Relieving pain and increasing relaxation in their clients while moving energy along their bodies and aligning their chakras. Alternatively, they can do healing work that does not involve physical touch. These lightworkers can administer natural medicine in the form of herbs, spices, and oils from various regions and cultures. Some may use stones and crystals as conduits to channel the universe's healing energy or absorb negative energy.

Healing Vocations

If you are a lightworker whose purpose is to heal the planet, you can be an environmental activist. This can be a small project where you help clean up the streets and beaches on the weekend. Have a local drive where you teach people about recycling and how they integrate that into their lives. You could do this alongside your regular job, which pays your bills. Or you could commit yourself to something bigger, like working with international organizations and nonprofits to finance research on climate change. You could even work as an environmental lawyer, litigating against corporations who contribute to the world's massive carbon emissions.

Other lightworkers are called to teach and share spiritual truths and lessons with other souls. Some may choose to teach practices that align the mind, body, and spirit through meditative movement.

For example, a lightworker may decide to teach Tai Chi, a form of martial arts which teaches both meditative movement and self-defense tactics. It involves deep breathing and slow movements that effortlessly flow into each other. While doing Tai Chi, you can cultivate energy known as qi and feel as it moves through your body, bringing your mind and body into harmony. In Chinese philosophy, qi is the life force that flows through all things and all people, binding us all together.

There are different styles of Tai Chi that they can choose to teach, with some being practiced more than others. Here are five main styles—The Chen, Yang, Wu, Wu/Hao, and Sun styles. There are also lesser practiced styles, such as Li, Fu, and Zhaobao. Each style is named after the instructor who created it or the village where it was developed. The five main techniques can be described accordingly:

- The Chen style is the original style of Tai Chi and has 83 movements. Its teachings focus on explosive power known as fa jin. They have movements that mix stomps and jumps, soft and hard movements, torso rotation, fast and slow movements, and heaving breathing.
- The Yang style has 108 movements and does not teach explosive power. It focuses on slow, large, and gentle movements with a wide stance and flexible knees.
- The Wu/Hao style uses a narrow stance with high postures and has complex techniques and circular motions.
- The Wu style has 84 movements, and most of its movements require you to lean the torso back and forth. Its stances are narrower than the Yang style, and it uses square postures and pushed hands.
- The Sun style is the gentlest one, using high postures, light footwork, and soft, fluid movements.

As you can see, each style comes with varying physical

demands, so a lightworker can make an informed decision on which to practice based on their physical capacity.

Another practice that utilizes meditative movement is yoga. A lightworker can train to become a certified yogi and join or open their own yoga practice. They help others heal their bodies and connect to their higher selves through an alignment of their mind, body, and spirit. As with Tai Chi, there are multitudes of yoga practices available, all with varying levels of difficulty and physical demand.

Not everyone is called to teach through physical practices. Some lightworkers may desire to teach and impart truths through tarot and psychic readings. Psychics are specialized types of lightworkers and are known as oracles, seers, or mediums. They are gifted with a keen intuition and sharpened senses, which allow them to communicate with other guides and spirits and guide all aspects of the client's life. Tarot readings make use of tarot card decks as a tool to provide specific insights on a focused area of the client's life. During tarot readings, the psychics will need to use their understanding of astrology, numerology, and other spiritual codes to decipher and interpret the messages on the cards before this. This, along with listening to their intuition, helps to relay an accurate reading to their clients. Both these readings use the same spiritual gift, so the lightworker will decide what they want to use based on the demand.

Artistic, Scientific, and Innovative Vocations

A lot of lightworkers find that they prefer to spread love and light through artistic means. You may find that most artists are healers, messengers, or divine lightkeepers. Some may use lyrics and musical frequencies to radiate positivity and light to people. Others may use paintings, videos, or other creative mediums to spread messages of hope, inspiration, and encouragement. Some write poems, essays, and blogs as a way to spread light, and some of these written works may even double as a tool for spiritual teachings. Lightworkers commercializing their artistic expression is a viable way to fulfill their purpose. Their work can spread joy and positivity, transmute dark emotions and radiate light to people worldwide. Artists use their work to communicate their understanding and perception of the universe to others. The creativity needed to do so come from their intuition, which they can only tap into when connected to their higher selves. This makes art a spiritual experience even when the subject of the work is not itself spiritual.

Some lightworkers are called to help humanity imagine a way of existence, push past our current society's limitations, and evolve. Those lightworkers can be found working as scientists and inventors, constantly testing what we know, helping us gain a deeper understanding of scientific laws and principles. It may seem counterintuitive for a spiritually awakened person to pursue scientific study because scientists almost always deny the validity of spirituality. Still, science explains universal truths in a way that the human can comprehend. There are numerous occasions where a scientific discovery confirms what spiritualists have claimed for decades. It only makes sense that some lightworkers might be drawn towards a field of study that tries to understand ideas and aspects of humanity that we are not yet privy to and share this knowledge with others to enlighten them.

Other lightworkers are called to pursue justice and to help make our world one of equality and integrity. These are the people we may find working in the justice system. Pushing for reform or as lawyers defending ordinary people from the rich and powerful or as diplomats involved in brokering peace between nations. They are lightworkers whose calling is to reduce the number of negative vibrations in the world to increase the capacity for light to radiate. These lightworkers are often neutralizers and divine lightkeepers.

There are lightworkers whose purpose is best fulfilled in a particular field. In contrast, others can work anywhere, as long as the work does not deplete their energy to the point that they cannot go out and do any lightwork. People need to be in touch with their higher self to know what kind of lightworker they are and their purpose. Furthermore, they need to communicate with their guides and angels, who will help them navigate the daily choices they will need to make as they go about fulfilling their purpose. Lightworkers are called to live full and bold lives and need to completely surrender themselves to their particular divine template. It goes without saying that the more connected they are to their higher selves, the more success they will attract to whichever vocation they choose to follow.

If they choose to follow their purpose, they need to consistently focus their minds on a higher perspective. It's effortless for a lightworker to become so concerned with earthly things that they veer off the paths meant to help them balance their physical and material needs.

THREE

Types of Lightworkers

"IT IS GOOD TO HAVE AN END TO JOURNEY TOWARD; BUT IT IS THE journey that matters, in the end." -Ursula K. LeGuin

Now that we've discussed the kind of work done by lightworkers, we can move on to the different types of lightworkers in the world. While it's true that some lightworkers may be guided into specific professions, which allow them to maximize their impact, they are mostly free to do any sort of work. As long as it does not prevent them from staying connected to their higher selves.

To fulfill your purpose as a lightworker, you must know the kind of lightworker you are. This will allow you to understand what spiritual gifts and talents you have, your mission here on earth, and which traits will help you on your mission.

Lightworkers require different levels of Ascension to access their spiritual gifts and talents. Specific skills harness energy and information within exact dimensions, so lightworkers need to reach the level of awakening that coincides with the dimension in which their gifts operate best.

There is some disagreement in the spiritual community on how many dimensions exist within the universe and on what exactly happens or is possible in each one. In general, there is an agreement that there are at least seven dimensions in the universe. I will only be dealing with the first five, as they're the ones relevant to the work done by lightworkers. All dimensions are within the same space and time, but some are not immediately perceivable to our senses. As third or fourth dimensions beings, we can only perceive the first three dimensions. They are measured in ways our senses "see" and understand (length, breadth, and height). We can also perceive the fourth dimension of time because we are aware of its effects. We see the sun as it rises and sets and see the leaves on a tree blossom and wilt. Some people can access the fourth dimension through their "sixth sense" before they are even awakened. They have a strong intuition and suddenly gain an understanding or knowledge about something seemingly out of nowhere. Guides, angels, and our higher selves communicate within the fourth dimension, so that sense of knowing a person suddenly receives is the communication from these beings.

Suppose we want to raise our vibrations and access higher dimensions. In that case, we need to focus our consciousness on becoming aware of them. This is why meditation is a great way to boost your consciousness. It helps you expand your focus from the first dimension, where you are in total stillness and only aware of yourself. Before this extends to being aware of your surroundings, your thoughts, and the energy that flows within you and around you. Lower dimensions are more rooted in the understanding of being separated from everything. Higher dimensions have a stronger sense of connectedness between beings because of their proximity to the spirit. When we begin the journey towards Ascension, our consciousness can intentionally transcend the limitations of our dimension. At the same time, our physical beings remain rooted in it. This is how people can get in touch with their guides and have lucid dreams while occupying their physical bodies. The former is an example of accessing the fourth dimension while physically awake. The latter is an example of accessing that realm while being physically asleep. Ascended masters and those granted wisdom by the universe explain the different dimensions in the following way.

The first dimension is an awareness of our physical selves only. You are only aware of the singularity of your existence. You have no individual identity because there is no need for a descriptor that distinguishes you from anything else. Crystals are one-dimensional objects because they are only aware of their existence, even though they are great amplifiers of energy from other realms.

The second dimension houses our emotional selves. We are aware of a blanket separation between ourselves and everything else in the universe in this realm. Being in this dimension is like being in a room and only being aware of the separation between yourself and the room. You don't recognize the objects in the room as being separate from the room itself.

The third dimension is where our awareness of the separation between ourselves and other things deepens. We can now distinguish the objects in the room as separate from the room itself and start interacting with them. This is the dimension that our planet vibrates in. Our ego-minds develop in this dimension based on what they can perceive with their senses. This determines how they choose to interact with different things.

The fourth dimension is where our higher self-resides—where we experience thoughts, emotions, intuition, imagination, and the passing of time. All of these things exist beyond what the ego-mind can perceive, although we feel and experience them. Matter still exists here, but it is easier to manipulate than in the third dimension. The fourth dimension is the core frequency for most lightworkers because they can connect with their higher self and transcend the limited physical perception of the earth. This realm is particularly powerful for dreamers, seers, and messengers. Dreamers can experience different timelines through this realm. Seers have their psychic gifts from this realm. Messengers get information from their guides and angels in this realm.

The fifth dimension is the highest dimension that our physical beings have access to. It is the realm in which our egos and shadows have come into perfect harmony, and our souls are whole again. We understand the exceptional integration of all that is in existence in this realm. We can still exist within our physical bodies, but our perception is no longer limited by our senses. Gatekeepers and ascension guides have access to the fifth dimension as beings who have achieved total enlightenment. When you have ascended into this dimension, you no longer experience lower frequencies.

Now that you understand the different realms and how each one works, let's look at the different kinds of lightworkers and their purpose.

The Gatekeepers

Gatekeepers are lightworkers who have completed their ascension experience and ultimately reunited their souls. These are beings who have achieved total enlightenment and operate within the fifth dimension. Instead of progressing to the next level of existence, they choose to remain in their physical bodies to share the knowledge of Ascension with others. Show them how to ascend through the various levels of consciousness. They carry divine wisdom and light in their bodies.

Consequently, their presence on this plane helps keep the ascension portal open while grounding the earth and raising its vibrations. Gatekeepers are usually not perceivable to people who have not begun their spiritual awakening because of the quantity of light they carry. Ascension can be mentally and spiritually overwhelming, and many people struggle to balance life on earth with their spiritual awakening. Gatekeepers help those undergoing a spiritual awakening by keeping the ascension portals open.

They also work in groups to keep the earth's grid and ley lines open and protected. They work to reopen closed interdimensional gateways and create new ones across the planet. The universe passes energy and information along through electromagnetic waves that are channeled through various grids. Gatekeepers give information and energy primarily along the earth's crystalline grid and the Heart grid. The Crystalline grid channels the universe's energy at different dimensions through crystals. Because crystals are located all over the earth and carry their frequencies, they can amplify this energy and send it across the planet. The Heart grid is what connects our hearts. The ego blocks our access to this grid when it takes charge of our consciousness. However, when we awaken and connect to our higher selves, we reconnect to the heart grid. These grids help the universe transfer energy and information across dimensions harmoniously while connecting us all.

Traits of a Gatekeeper

Gatekeepers are generally helpful and don't mind giving their time to do something for someone else. They love harmony and peace and want to help create a just and fair world, where everyone is treated equally and not shunned for living authentically. Gatekeepers are often kind souls who radiate a trusting warmth. As ascended beings, gatekeepers understand spiritual truths and readily share this knowledge with others. Gatekeepers embody bliss, love, and gratitude because they know the deep connections we all have with each other and have access to the universe's complete unconditional love. They are not argumentative because they know that there is no separation between anything and that everything can only obey the universal truth. With this awareness comes a loss for the need to be right or to compete for anything. This awareness is what makes them natural peacemakers. They know that once we can transcend our sensory desire for competition, we come closer to being united with Source and the spirit.

The Healers

Healers are lightworkers who alleviate the pain of any living thing they encounter—souls, plants, animals, and even the planet itself. They usually have a heightened pain sensitivity and can sense someone who isn't aware of their pain yet. Healers always have traumatic and turbulent lives. To effectively fulfill their purpose, they need to be healed from the traumas they have experienced. This way, they can connect to their higher selves, tap into their light, and use it to heal others. This also allows them to heal others with a deep sense of compassion, having gone through similar experiences themselves.

Healers fulfill their purpose across a wide variety of spheres, including physically and mentally. This enables healers to work either in the third or fourth dimension, depending on the work they have to perform. Each healer uses different tools and techniques to heal. They need to be in touch with their intuition to listen for guidance from their guides and angels on the most effective ways to utilize their skills.

Traits of a Healer

Healers are compassionate, warm beings who are drawn to help others. They can usually sense when someone's energy is low because they are battling some kind of pain. If they are also empaths, they feel people's emotional pain as their own. They can differentiate between hidden agendas from genuine expressions. Healers are also called to heal the planet and nature, so they feel deep remorse at destroying natural habitats and the abuse of animals.

The Messengers

Messengers are lightworkers who receive messages from their higher self, ascended masters, the universe, and angels. They then pass these messages to humanity. They spread messages of love, peace, and guidance. Messengers often work as writers, motivational speakers, artists, musicians, and spiritual teachers. They spread the information they've received through websites, books, movies, and various other platforms where accessibility is made easier. Messengers need to be in touch with their consciousness because these messages are communicated through their intuition. If they are not present and aware, they can miss the communication. This also helps the messengers to differentiate between words from the spirit and those from the ego. Messengers work primarily in the fourth dimension because they communicate mostly with beings that are not perceivable in the physical realm.

Traits of a Messenger

They have a presence that commands attention, and their aura is gentle yet authoritative. These attributes help them to attract an audience and for their messages to be taken seriously and with acceptance. Messengers are usually creative beings, able to present the universe's communication in a way that people can easily understand without watering it down.

The Seers

Seers are also known as oracles or psychics. They have their third eye opened and have a strong intuition. If you are a Seer, your knowledge and wisdom come from your higher self, angel guides, and spirit guides. Your higher self communicates with you primarily through your intuition because your guides are in constant and direct communication with this self. You can see beyond the perceived natural reality and into various timelines at once. Seers mainly work in the fourth dimension because their spiritual gifts of intuition and communication with other beings are strongest. Their abilities allow them to see the future and manifest it into the physical realm because, like any person, their thoughts eventually become their actions. This is why Seers have manifesting abilities that are stronger than the average lightworker. Seers also work in the third dimension when communicating their knowledge to others through various forms of divination, most commonly through psychic and tarot readings. As lightworkers, their goal is to promote peace and provide encouragement and security for their readings. A common misconception is that all seers can communicate with deceased spirits.

Most Seers only have access to divine information, which is provided by their guides. Only some of them can communicate directly with the deceased in the physical plane. The dead will probably communicate with them through their spirit-mind using thoughts, emotions, and intuition for those who can.

Traits of a Seer

Seers are some of the most spiritually gifted lightworkers. They can have visions that later happen in the physical world exactly how they saw them. They can sense the presence of a spirit in any environment because their bodies react to them. They can feel the energy radiating from other people and discern if it is positive or negative. This is especially helpful during readings because it allows their intuition to communicate with the other person's higher self. They hear messages from their guides or their higher self through their physical or spiritual ear. Seers can sometimes communicate telepathically with other spirits, even if they are in different dimensions from each other. Lastly, seers can have intimate knowledge of a situation or even know random things without any previous context or awareness of the matter.

The Neutralizers

I like to think of neutralizers as the firefighters amongst the lightworkers, extinguishing the world's dark energy flames. A neutralizer's purpose is slightly different from a normal lightworker's because sharing light energy with others is not their primary function. They are called to neutralize dark light from the earth and usually work with transmuters, turning this neutralized energy into light energy. Because their work requires them to tackle darkness head-on and neutralize it. Their light energy is used mainly to protect their energy field from absorbing any darkness. A neutralizer creates an increased capacity for light energy to enter the planet, which helps raise the collective consciousness. They can be found working in dispute resolution, peace-building, diplomacy, and other areas that require the skill of neutralizing high-tension situations.

Traits of a Neutralizer

Neutralizers are often very calm people who are not easily riled up by external conflict or chaos. They are people who can work under pressure and think in straightforward, easy-to-follow ways. They know how to find the easiest and nearest solution to complex matters.

The Dreamers

Dreamers are known to challenge social norms and encourage inter-dimensional change. They often have lucid dreams filled with symbolic imagery and hidden messages from the universe. They write their dreams down and meditate on them during their moments of mindfulness. In this space of awareness, they can interpret any symbolism and imagery in their dreams to better understand them. Some dreamers can travel to different dimensions in their dreams to learn about different ways of existing to help our planet implement them.

These dreamers can astrally project out of their bodies and access earth's grid lines so that they can use its frequencies to travel to other planes of existence. Whether they are lucid dreamers or astral projectors, both are fully conscious and aware of their kind of experience. This is why they can actively interact with other souls and astral beings in their dreams, ask questions and learn. They can also manipulate matter and build new realities in their dreams. Their gift operates in the fourth dimension.

Traits of a Dreamer

Dreamers are creative, innovative, and know-how to think out of the box. They are deeply connected to their intuition. Dreamers are confident and assertive, a trait that serves them well when trying to push the boundaries of human thought in the physical realm. It helps them be taken seriously as they propose new and outlandish ways of being.

The Adventurers

Adventurers are called to help humanity evolve and create better future realities. They are constantly exploring and are not afraid to reach new frontiers. They want to advance humanity to a new level of being by raising their collective consciousness. They do this by pushing them past their imagined limits and closer to their highest selves. They know how to encourage people, especially in their moments of crisis.

Traits of an Adventurer

Like dreamers, adventurers are visionaries who think outside the box and are not afraid of the unknown. These are people who are regarded as thought leaders and game-changers in our society. Many adventurers are entrepreneurial because they can identify areas that can use an advancement or a complete overhaul in society.

The Manifestors

Manifestors are lightworkers who channel energy at their level of consciousness to manifest positivity for the planet and the people they interact with. For most Manifestors, their purpose is realized passively. All they do is focus on maintaining their level of consciousness and absorbing light energy. This alone is enough to manifest peace and love for the planet's good and attract positivity for themselves and other people. However, some are actively fulfilling their purpose by manifesting particular things. Manifestors are very powerful. They must take heed not to get drawn into darkness, manifesting things only for personal and material gain and not for the good of humanity. Manifestors work in the fourth dimension. Their thoughts are their most powerful gift because whatever they think of faster than other people wherever they attract.

Traits of a Manifestor

Manifestors have an innate awareness that whatever they think about or focus their energy on eventually comes to them. This awareness is true for all of them, even those yet to be awakened and fully come into their power. Manifestors who have a hard time controlling their thoughts try to always immerse themselves in some sort of distraction or hyperactivity. They are constantly plugged into their headphones, always busy with some or other commitments. They do whatever it takes to stop themselves from having a moment where their thoughts can run wild. Of course, this is counterproductive because this fear of their power will manifest in their personal lives.

The Transmuters

Transmuters are called to dispel negative, dark energy and transform it into light energy. They absorb and transform this energy into light and radiate it back into the earth. This then raises the planet's collective consciousness. As mentioned before, transmuters often work with neutralizers. Transmuters can also help families to break generational curses by transforming the energy generated by ancestral negative karma and trauma into the light. Ancestral trauma occurs when people in a generation experience an alarming trauma and do not work to resolve its effects. This creates dark energy, which is then passed down through generations, becoming more entrenched as time passes. Things continue in this fashion until someone in the family chooses to tackle the problem and resolve it. This often requires them to do shadow work by confronting fears, habits, and perceptions passed down. Transmuters help to make this process easier on an energy level. Transmuters usually choose to be reincarnated into such families. They are then the ones who clear their family's dark karma.

Transmuters understand that energy can be changed from one form to another. Everything is always in a state of motion. They tap into this constant flux when transmuting energy. Like Manifestors, they understand that our thoughts will eventually move into the physical world. This happened because repeated thoughts stir up emotions expressed through the body, acting on these, bringing the idea into reality. Transmuters also use thoughts to manifest positive change for mankind and the planet, although this always happens subconsciously for them. They neutralize dark energy by confronting it and radiating light onto it.

Traits of a Transmuter

Transmuters are good at forgiving others and spreading positivity at all times, especially in the midst of great chaos. They are good at identifying people's negative traits and helping them to transform these into something positive. Transmuters make great therapists. They have an exceptional talent for encouraging, inspiring, and guiding people towards fully stepping into their power. Transmuters radiate positivity and love.

The Divine Lightkeepers

Divine Lightkeepers are lightworkers who are called to constantly radiate light into the world. Unlike transmuters, they don't transform dark energy into light. They play a key role in raising the collective consciousness by being a reliable embodiment of light, even during utter chaos. Unlike gatekeepers, divine lightkeepers are usually solitary and do their lightwork independently. Because they are a constant conduit of light, they need to always be present and aware. This makes divine lightkeepers the most reclusive kind of lightworker. Their solitary nature helps them minimize their interactions with dark energy.

Traits of a Divine Lightkeeper

Divine Lightkeepers are known to be kind and are always helping others. Their energy field is welcoming and draws people in, allowing them to spread their light. They are always spreading positivity, even unconsciously. A divine lightkeeper's mere presence radiates joy, and people are automatically happier and lighter when they are around them. Their calling requires them to have an energy field that is always open and radiating light. It is their nature to practice things that raise their consciousness. Autonomous in nature, selfless, and compassionate. They are the kind of people that always look for the bright side of every experience. They don't often form deep, meaningful connections with other people like healers do. They often perform random acts of kindness for strangers.

The Ascension Guides

Ascension guides are lightworkers who have undergone spiritual Ascension and chose to guide others on their journey of

Ascension. Their early lives are often marked by experiences that are more traumatic than the average lightworker. The struggles they face as they do their shadow work and raise their consciousness to inform their approach to guiding others. They usually felt abandoned during their most significant moments of adversity, which inspires them to help others. Part of this help includes showing humanity that there is always more than one way to do things. When people understand this, their ascension journey becomes easier because they search for alternative perspectives to their problems instead of giving up.

They help other souls to stay on the path to consciousness by offering encouragement when things get complicated. This makes them great spiritual mentors and teachers. Unlike other lightworkers, they are conscious of their purpose and don't fulfill it passively. Their guidance is deeply informed by their own experiences and the knowledge they receive directly from the universe. As such, many of what they do or teach may seem to contradict the teachings of people who have not undergone Ascension themselves. The only difference between gatekeepers and ascension guides is that gatekeepers work to keep interdimensional gateways and portals open in addition to their work as guides for those undergoing a spiritual awakening.

Traits of an Ascension Guide

Ascension guides are people who are kind and compassionate and strive to always lend a helping hand. They exude positivity, and their aura is welcoming, making it easy for people to trust them. They live spiritually authentic lives and are not afraid to question and even contradict popular discourse around matters of spirituality. They bring a fresh perspective and understanding of the process of Ascension.

The Way Showers

Way Showers are similar to Ascension Guides in that they guide others through their journey to awakening. However, their guidance is focused more on the physical world. They are the people who live eccentrically, who are unafraid to live boldly and without fear of what others will say. Way Showers are in touch with their authentic inner selves and teach others how to live authentically. They are honest about the challenges of living as an awakened spiritual being in the physical world. They inspire others to live and love themselves and others with compassion and understanding. They are not afraid to challenge social conventions. Way Showers are called to help create a new world where we all live together in harmony. People are unafraid to live as their most authentic selves without the fear of being chastised or ostracized for it. They, too, imagine a world of equality and a true sense of community. In this way, their work is similar to that of Adventurers and Dreamers.

Traits of a Way Shower

Way Showers are often the first people in their families to undergo a spiritual awakening. They tend to be completely different from the rest of the clan. They see things from a higher perspective and are peaceful and nurturing because of it. Their connection to their higher selves makes them exude love and light. Their aura attracts people who require guidance. These are the people that society considers to be "free spirits."

The Divine Blueprint Holders

Divine Blueprint Holders have special access to the divine template of every person's fully enlightened self. Their purpose is to translate and share this template with others. Before our souls are reincarnated on this plane, our higher self agrees with our guides and the spirit on the kind of life we'd like to lead on earth in service of the greater good. The blueprint template contains exact details regarding the type of life we are meant to live in our most authentic form. It gives you an outline of your likes and dislikes, personality, and family. It sets out exactly your purpose and who you can communicate with to help realize your fullest potential. Each person has an innate awareness of what their fully awakened self would be like. Still, most people struggle to access this knowledge because of their physical form's limitations on their soul's ability to reconnect.

Divine Blueprint Holders know how to use sacred tools such as geometry and the akashic records to interpret and understand each person's divine template. The akashic records are the universe's filing and storage system, keeping records of everything that ever has and ever will happen across all planes of existence. On the other hand, sacred geometry is the study of how the universe's fundamental geometric shapes are used to create the energy patterns that flow through everything in existence, uniting us all. Divine Blueprint Holders don't actively fulfill their mission because they don't directly tell others the best way to live their lives. Instead, they manifest this knowledge through the words and actions they employ as they go about their daily lives.

Traits of a Divine Blueprint Holder

Divine Blueprint Holders are good at identifying people's hidden talents and usually guide them towards exploring them. They exhibit a deep understanding of the universe's inner workings and are often very intellectual. Many Divine Blueprint Holders are mathematically gifted and end up working as scientists, actuaries, and inventors.

FOUR

The Four Pillars of Lightworkers

"OUR DEEPEST FEAR IS NOT THAT WE ARE INADEQUATE. OUR deepest fear is that we are powerful beyond measure. It is our Light, not our Darkness that frightens us." -Maryanne Williamson

Do you regularly read blogs about spirituality, well-being, and expanding your consciousness? Chances are that you might be a lightworker. There is just something about these driven souls that keeps the world going. Michael Mirdad first coined the term *"Lightworker"* during the early 80s. Then, Doreen Virtue launched *"The Lightworkers Way"* in 1997, which became an instant hit.

Suppose you are wondering who is a lightworker. In that case, anyone who feels an enormous pull towards helping other people is a lightworker. Such individuals are also known as star seeds, earth angels, indigos, and crystal babies. These spiritual beings provide our planet with a beacon of hope. They are committed to serving humanity. From the moment they are born, they tend to be compassionate and kind. In fact, lightworkers start rescuing animals and other living beings from a very young age.

Known for being highly sensitive, lightworkers sense the anguish and sadness others feel around them and cannot just sit back and watch. They gravitate to favor occupations and careers that allow them to express their empathetic style. You will come across lightworkers who pursue a career in nursing, rehabilitation, therapy, teaching, research, veterinary services, caregiving, healing, and the like. They follow internal guidance and are highly intuitive. As they can perceive the emotions of other living beings, they direct their healing powers towards helping others. They strive to chase away and dispel negative consciousness with their vibrant energy and healing power.

Now, every lightworker doesn't need to realize their nature or spiritual calling. Even though some star seeds might come to understand their purpose to elevate the collective consciousness of mankind, many do not.

The following four pillars will help one identify being a lightworker.

Heal Yourself to Heal Others

The first pillar of lightworkers is their ability to heal themselves and then heal others. They know who they are and can pursue a mission of great healing. Even though most lightworkers tend to navigate spirituality, they don't need to consistently follow their healing path. Even if one reads all the books in the world about metaphysical concepts, they might not live according to such ideas. Only when you embody the wisdom of your infinite soul are you able to truly heal.

During the first years of your awakening, you might feel like you can understand everything. You would feel like you are mastering your mind. It is possible that your inner child healing has worked. Thus, you would start to notice things coming together nicely. As your soil is guided to its calling, the universe would go above and beyond to provide you with unlimited support. This is only the beginning of every lightworker's mission. Park of your mission is to heal your soul's journey.

There are various stages of healing. Therefore, you should never rush it. However, you must ensure that your journey continues. You must lay a firm foundation. You must understand that your ego would get more innovative, too, as you evolve. It might mislead you into believing that you cannot completely heal the past traumas of life. You must stay committed to deep soul healing.

Integrate Parallel Versions

Next, you have to integrate parallel versions of yourself. You will start to notice that your relationship with time would change entirely. Lightworkers realize that they can expand or collapse timeliness. You get to withdraw knowledge from every aspect of reality and connect with different versions of your potential future, parallel future, present future, and past. The second pillar requires you to integrate many of your gifts and memories of different lives. Then, you move towards a cosmic level of integration. This is when your mission would begin to make sense at last. Always remember that each soul has a purpose. As you realize this, you would get to master your soul.

Be In Service to Others

Once you realize your mission as a lightworker, you will start to become of service to others. Healing and unraveling your life will enable you to recognize that you have trained to be in service to others for thousands of years. The journey of your soul is intertwined with others. You have a soul contract with every person you come into contact with. You help them heal and awaken. Now, you must be wondering if you need to help others as a lightworker.

The unique design of your soul will guide you to be of service to others in a distinct way. Some lightworkers are the best crystal keepers. They access information that has been stored in crystals from the beginning of time. Other lightworkers would help and protect plants and animals. In contrast, some would work with children to ensure that they maintain their gifts and purity. You will be guided to become a teacher at some point. It is valid for each lightworker. It all boils down to your independent attitude and your own soul contract.

Spiritual Leadership

Finally, the last pillar of lightworkers is spiritual leadership. When we talk about leadership, it does not mean being in a superior position. Instead, it simply refers to a deep commitment towards the path of self-mastery. Thus, you get to teach others your divinity. By stepping into your spiritual leadership, you grow exponentially. It will challenge you to do the impossible. You will notice spiritual tests and miracles pouring into your life and leading you towards mastery.

At any point in time, each lightworker would be asked to become a spiritual leader. Once you are called, you would be guided to work with others. You might feel overwhelmed initially. However, it is the right path for you as you had chosen it. It should feel natural even if it does not seem easy. Your life would be an open book as you continue to practice self-mastery. Being in service to others is what being a lightworker is about. Only when you help yourself would you be able to help others.

Master the earthly plane by stepping into what your soul was meant to be. Move towards a more galactic role and illuminate the path of every person you encounter. As you ascend towards mastery, everything will fall into place.

FIVE

Seven Signs You May Be a Lightworker

"THE BEST WAY TO FIND YOURSELF IS TO LOSE YOURSELF IN THE service of others." -Mahatma Gandhi

We live in a world where the actions of others play a role in either furthering or hindering our personal goals. It is to be expected that many people will want to help others because they understand that this directly or indirectly has a positive effect on themselves. This effect may come in various forms, such as feeling better about themselves, "balancing the scales" by making up for something harmful they did beforehand, or protecting their interests in one way or another. This does not mean that everyone who does good deeds is a lightworker. Lightworkers are more concerned with doing good for the sake of mankind.

Lightworkers are souls who agreed to come down to earth to spread light, positivity and to unite mankind with Source once more. They tend not to focus on how their good deeds will affect their futures. Lightworkers understand that there is bliss to be found in every experience, even if it's not particularly enjoyable. There is a difference in the intentions behind the good deeds of a lightworker and someone who is not. Therefore, it is important to discern between people operating from an ego-mind reality and those on a spiritual mission to bring light and love and raise the collective consciousness. This is not to say that people who do good for the sake of personal gain are bad, just that the effect of the good deeds of a lightworker is far greater.

Lightworkers Are Healers

Lightworkers gain a sense of fulfillment from helping and healing themselves and others. You are often drawn to pedagogies that focus on fixing, improving, and innovating ways of life, both for the environment and society. As you may remember, I spoke of healers being a specific type of lightworker whose purpose is to heal humans, animals, and the planet through various techniques. This is not the kind of healing I mean here. Lightworkers are called to heal and inspire humanity towards the light. This is a general trait that informs the work of any lightworker, regardless of whether you are a seer, gatekeeper, or any other type. This is why all lightworkers are subjected to difficult and often traumatic life experiences you need to heal before you can step into your higher self. The work of a lightworker is multi-tiered because humanity is scarred in a plethora of ways. As such, you are drawn to healing in the physical, mental, spiritual, and emotional spheres.

Before embarking on your mission to heal humanity and its planet, you must first channel inner healing. What's important to note here is that healing is a lifelong affair. Some wounds are so deep and dark that you just have to learn how to carry them with you on your life journey. Other injuries and traumas can resurface as trigger points while trying to heal or help someone else. This is normal, so don't worry when something like this happens. One of the strengths you will have as a healer is knowing how to heal yourself when you are triggered or when you fall into the trap of destructive habits. As a lightworker, you will learn the best methods to regulate your emotions and build boundaries to keep unwanted energy away from your aura.

You Trust in Spiritual Practices

The basis of a lightworker's purpose has a spiritual nature. So it makes sense that you are drawn towards practices that help you access and understand that part of yourself better. People in the world can go their entire lives without venturing into any kind of spirituality, but you are not like that. You know that spirituality is an integral part of any fulfilled life. You probably feel off-kilter when you are not exploring your spirituality. Lightworkers tend to be drawn towards spiritual practices that focus on energies, the connectedness of all beings, and understanding their inner power. Because you are often social outcasts or prefer to spend time away from others, you may find yourself gravitating away from organized religion due to its institutional, group-based nature. This aligns with your commitment towards personal growth because, in organized religion, the focus tends to shift very quickly from personal growth to religiously following rules and doctrine. Spiritual practices allow you to access a sense of purpose and feel connected to a higher power personally.

Because of your spiritual inclinations, you can often discern which practices resonate with your spirit and which do not. You have an innate understanding that there is order to the universe and that you have an important place within it. You are the kind of person that is good at selecting which spiritual and religious teachings you want to rely on because you understand that each religion reflects a modicum of truth. You essentially craft your own spiritual guidance manual.

This manual plays an important role in building the foundation of teaching you how to harness the light and be aligned with your most authentic self. After you have awakened and are moving towards complete alignment with Source, the universe's instructions to you regarding how to grow and fulfill your purpose effectively will come more directly during your moments of stillness and connectedness with your intuition. You will no longer need to rely so heavily on the spiritual truths as told by other people. Your angels and guides will communicate these to you in a way that makes unique sense to you.

Lightworkers Are Natural Manifestors

You can naturally envision something that is not yet a reality, focus on it, and receive it from the universe. This happens without you having to exert much effort towards this cause. You understand that everything is energy and that you attract things on the same wavelength as your frequency. Manifesting, in this sense, is less about asking the universe for material and financial gain. It's more about asking for the things that will put you in a position where you are best able to fulfill your purpose.

Manifesting as a lightworker, however, is not about feeding our pride and personal wants. It's more aligned with our deepest human desire: To live in love, light, and unity with the universe. Of course, some lightworkers succumb to their egos and only manifest things that bring them personal grain. Lightworkers need to intentionally resist this by continually raising their consciousness and moving away from the desire to live a life fueled by sensory desires. Manifestation is not a magical vending machine. It is about being conscious of your energies. Asking Source to bring you the things that will help you care for your needs and execute your mission during that specific period.

Most people think they can trick the universe into providing them with things that feed their ego while living from a perspective of fear and lack. This is why so many think that manifestation does not work for them. You can only attract what you believe. If you don't believe you are meant to live in abundance, you won't attract things that vibrate along the same wavelength as abundance.

You Always Seek the Truth and Deeper Meaning

Lightworkers are inquisitive and have a philosophical outlook on life. You are very self-aware and are always on a quest to understand how your experiences relate to those of others and what underlying truths this can reveal. Your inquisitive nature makes you prone to do things that other people might find too dangerous or outlandish. Still, you want to understand what people gain from these experiences, so you readily join in on them. You want to know what your purpose is and how you can live a fulfilled life. This desire goes beyond material fulfillment.

Your search for universal truths in the knowledge available to you. As such, you are often drawn to the sciences, philosophy, anthropology, and other such pedagogies. You understand that there is more to life than the humdrum of everyday life and the social norms that constrict mankind. Lightworkers have a niggling sense that there is a higher, universal truth that our physical bodies do not allow us to perceive. They want to pierce the veil and see behind the facade.

Sensitivity Is Essential in Lightworkers

Lightworkers are conduits of light energy, which means their energy fields are more sensitive than most people's. As a lightworker, you can detect energy shifts within a space or a person because you act as a lightning rod for energy. Your sensitivity extends to your own emotions as well, so chances are that you are easily offended, and you cry easily. You are probably the kind of person to cry while watching an emotional scene in a movie or reading a heartwarming piece in a blog or a magazine column.

Some lightworkers are also empaths, meaning that they resonate with emotions as much as they do with energies. If you fall within this category, you can understand the feelings of others on a deep level. Their feelings can affect your moods because your sensitivity means you absorb these feelings alongside their energies. As such, you will feel light and happy when you are around people who are experiencing light emotions like joy, happiness, and contentment. You will also feel drained and burdened around those with dark emotions or thoughts like bitterness, jealousy, and fear. Empathetic lightworkers can detect false emotions and discern hidden agendas. This goes a long way in building genuine connections with others because it makes them feel seen and valued, making them more receptive to getting help from you. This trait can also make you resented by people who like to manipulate others for their own benefit. Still, it will come to serve you well once you learn to stop naively believing that everyone genuinely wants help.

Unfortunately, empathic lightworkers are often bleeding hearts, wanting to help everyone in sight. You may have difficulties setting or asserting boundaries with others. You may frequently find yourself overwhelmed by the energies around you and need to disconnect from the world for some time. This also means that it's easy for people to take advantage of you, especially when you are spiritually young and have not yet learned how to set boundaries and master your gifts. Self-care is essential for lightworkers because it prevents them from exerting themselves beyond their capacity.

You Feel Close to Nature

A lightworker feels a close connection to nature. You have always felt a deep love and respect for animals and the natural environment alike. You probably prefer to live in a place surrounded by natural grass, trees, and flowers. Suppose you live in urban or city areas. In that case, your home probably more closely resembles a jungle than an apartment, with pot plants and hanging vines adorning as much space as possible. You honor animals and never intentionally harm them because you know that all life is equally valuable. You are probably a vegan because you are uncomfortable with the idea that animals are killed so that you can feed and clothe yourself.

Whenever you feel overwhelmed, you find yourself wanting to go out amongst the birds and trees. You enjoy feeling the sun on your face and the breeze on your body. You like the smell of freshly cut grass and looking at the different trees and flowers around you. You feel energized in this space because it is a way for your spirit to connect with Source outside of the chaos of civilization. When you are in nature, you can walk around barefoot and ground yourself. You can peacefully meditate and release any negative energy from your body. At the same time, you absorb the light energy from your surroundings.

Lightworkers are often adept at taking care of plants and animals. Many can be found working as vets, taking care of farm animals. You may find yourself volunteering at or leading organizations that focus on environmental conservation.

You May Be an Outcast or Loner

Lightworkers have open energy fields, which makes them sensitive to the energies of others. This often leaves you drained and causes you to isolate yourself from others so that you can recharge. You may have always felt at odds with your family, friends, and peers that you never quite fit in, and this makes you a social outcast. You see the world differently from others, and you are often misunderstood because of this. Because you tend to question things that others consider fundamental truths, your views and beliefs can attract controversy and conflict, which further isolates you. Ironically, your isolation leads to you having even more unique opinions. You are less influenced by what is socially acceptable when you are in your own world. You are averse to conflict because you understand that everything in the universe is meant to be in harmony. When you constantly feel confronted, you become withdrawn from most people, preferring to surround yourself with peaceful, in-depth interactions based on mutual respect and understanding.

Most times, lightworkers have a tough life and face challenges that most people don't have to deal with. This happens because the universe wants you to learn how to face darkness and overcome it. It's crucial for you to do this, as it helps you access your higher selves and because confronting and overcoming darkness is an integral part of the work of any lightworker. This is another reason why you may become a loner or a social outcast. Your life experiences can be of such a nature that you cannot interact with other people regularly. Perhaps you have controlling and abusive parents who monitor your every mood and decide who you may or may not speak to. Or maybe you have a physical ailment that limits your mobility. Or it could be that the effects of your experiences make you withdrawn from others, preferring to isolate yourself in your own world, which serves as your sanctuary.

Once you recognize these traits within yourself, you have to begin doing the shadow work to jumpstart your spiritual awakening. Let me reiterate again that the journey of a lightworker is not easy. Even as you become awakened and experience Ascension, you will still face hurdles that may tempt you to stop and return to the way of life you knew before. Many have chosen to remain asleep through this life because of fear. Others have embraced the darkness and become dark workers, focused on achieving their own goals and elevating themselves in this world. You need to set your intentions towards living a life that honors your purpose every day. You can still fall off the wayside as an awakened being, especially if you have not become enlightened at any level of Ascension. It's up to you to take the necessary measures to stay on the course towards unity with the spirit.

SIX

Self Care For the Lightworker

"THE HERO IS THE ONE WHO KINDLES A GREAT LIGHT IN THE world, who sets up blazing torches in the dark streets of life for men to see by. The saint is the man who walks through the dark paths of the world, himself a light." -Felix Adler

Lightworking is not easy work. You are constantly exposed to the energies of everything and everyone around you, whether good or bad. You have to find ways to help and heal people overcome by dark energies, even if they are resistant. This requires patience and for you to intentionally and consistently keep your ego and your shadow in harmony with one another. You must remain conscious of and aligned with your higher self so that you can keep your energy field as light and open as possible. Suppose you are overcome by dark energy and lose the connection to your higher frequency. In that case, your light dims, and your capacity to fulfill your purpose is severely limited. You need to set time aside and take care of your well-being. This is not just limited to your spiritual well-being. If you are not mentally, physically, and emotionally balanced, it's difficult for you to vibrate at a higher consciousness.

Each lightworker has methods that work best for them

because each one is different. If you are a new lightworker, it may take some time to figure out which method(s) work best for you. But don't fret about this. Be patient with yourself, try out as many different things as possible, and trust that the universe will reveal what is best for you. There are a few common ways to take care of your mental, physical, and spiritual well-being, and I will be sharing these with you here. Most of them require an acceptance and understanding of certain divine truths. This should be easy for you as an awakened being.

Clear Your Energy Field

Your energy field or aura is like a highway, constantly interacting with different energies as a lightworker. This can leave you feeling drained and overwhelmed. It is why you are sensitive and may need to take a moment to reflect on your day and release any unwanted energy. It's necessary to frequently clear your energy field so that it is not clogged. You can use any method to remove this unwanted energy. However, the most common and easiest ways are to do some physical movement or do things that spark joy within you, such as reading, cooking, or going to the movies.

Moving your body around is a great way to let old energy flow out of your body and new energy flow in. You can do some yoga and focus your mind on each energy and emotion you feel, analyze it, and decide if you will release it or retain it. Yoga provides an excellent release for stress, anxiety, and other low vibrational energies. The mindfulness that it requires helps you calm your mind and become aware of your thoughts and emotions. It allows you to think and reflect in a peaceful state, enabling you to make better decisions. Such decisions are not tainted by chaos and darkness.

If you want to combine this with your fitness regimen, you can do some high-intensity kinds of yoga or Tai Chi. Even just doing a regular cardio workout is excellent for clearing your energy field. Anything that makes you sweat out the toxins you've accumulated during the day will unclog your aura and leave you feeling spiritually and physically lighter.

You can also go for a meditative walk in nature and focus on how your body feels. Many lightworkers find that the fresh air helps them to clear their heads. If they walk barefoot, they can release any unwanted energy into the earth and fill the gap left behind by absorbing the light around them. Because you feel connected to nature, the experience of walking outside is much more spiritual for you than it is for others. A walk can also double as the perfect opportunity to meditate and say some positive and self-affirming mantras. When you are in this peaceful state of mind, you can communicate with your higher self, guides, and the Source for guidance and new knowledge.

Sound therapy is another excellent way to clear your energy field. You can try dancing, which is a fantastic way to release any tension in the body. The best way to do this is to just put on some music and start intuitively moving your body to the sounds. You will feel the energy move through you. If you start sweating, you can imagine that to be any unwanted energy leaving your body. Speaking of sounds, another great way to release energy is through clapping, singing, and drumming, using a singing bowl or you can try some throat singing. These methods have been used since time immemorial. They are great at raising the vibrations within yourself or in your environment. This is a great way to lighten your mood and quieting any dense thoughts and emotions. The different frequencies also help relieve stress, depression, and pain while maintaining mind and body harmony.

Another way to clear your energy field is to clean and organize your space. Any space you work in can quickly devolve into a chaotic mess. Taking time to clean and organize brings back a sense of order and light into your space. You may also find the act itself helps you think and tap into your consciousness because your mind is focused solely on the task at hand. You can amplify this by lighting candles with essential oil scents in the room. Essential oils have numerous protective and healing properties. You can use the light of fire itself to help dispel darkness from your space. Use scents such as lavender which is exceptional for clearing your mind and realigning you with your higher self. It's also known as one of the few oils that can help you unlock all your chakras because it promotes the flow of light energy.

Washing your body is also a great way to clear your energy field by washing off any dark energy. If you do work that requires you to physically touch people, it will help you wash your hands of the energies you have been absorbing throughout your day. You can also choose to immerse your entire body in water. Taking a bath with sea salt or Himalayan salt is a great way to purify your energy field. The salt attracts all the dark energy while drawing toxins out from the skin and stimulating the body's circulation. Alternatively, you can infuse the water with essential oils such as sage or eucalyptus, both of which are known to neutralize and purify dark energy.

You can also channel all unwanted energy into some form of artistic expression. You can paint, draw, or write about whatever comes to you when you think of the energy and emotions you want to get rid of. When you are done, you can destroy the piece and remove its residues from your space. Not only will this clear you of the emotions you no longer wanted to keep in your body, but it's also a very cathartic exercise.

Ground Yourself

The constant energetic stimuli that lightworkers are exposed to can leave you feeling untethered and unable to be fully present in any or all spheres of life. Grounding techniques help you be more present within yourself and connected to the earth. You can feel and understand all your emotions. Be fully aware of how your five senses interact to shape your experiences, and have the capacity to process and analyze your thoughts. It's important to always remain grounded because once you lose control and awareness of self; it's easy for everything to fall into a state of chaos. When you are grounded, your spiritual awareness is in harmony with physical awareness. This helps ensure that you don't become too focused on one area, leaving the other unattended.

There are several techniques you can employ to ground yourself. One of the best physical ways to ground yourself is by engaging your senses. A simple way to do this is by having a delicious meal. You can plate the food in an aesthetically pleasing way. Smell the different spices, savor the flavors. Enjoy the feeling of the food as it moves from your mouth, down your throat, and into your stomach. Or you can lie down and focus on your internal and external environment. Listen to the sounds around, to the aches in your body. When you do this, you become more present and can shut out any distracting thoughts or overwhelming emotions.

You can immerse yourself in creating a painting, a craft project, or anything of that nature. When you are creating, your physical presence is attributed to the motion of your body. In contrast, your mental and spiritual presence occurs as you focus your mind and spirit on bringing your creative vision to life.

Another great grounding technique is to start and end your day by journaling. You can write your goals and daily mantras down in the morning as you set your intentions for the day. End the day by reflecting on your thoughts and emotions that day.

You can also use a technique known as earthing, where you literally ground yourself to the earth. You'll need to walk barefoot against the soil or grass and get a more profound sense of connectivity to the earth. This is also a great way to release unwanted energy into the earth and absorb the light found amongst the trees and the birds.

You can also ground yourself by taking a hot shower, immediately turning on the cold water, and standing under it for a minute or two. This rapid temperature change will put your mind and body on high alert, so you will be fully present with yourself in those minutes. This is a great one to do if you are about to have a busy day because you don't have to add a new activity to your day.

If you want to do something quick to ground yourself, you can touch your face or arms and focus on the sensation. This helps to ground you, and it's a great way to soothe yourself and release tension from your body.

Connect With Your Intuition

Your intuition is your internal guidance. The thing that prepares you for situations you didn't even know you would encounter. It warns against the hidden dangers of this world and informs you of things beyond your physical knowledge. Suppose you are overextending yourself in your work, or you are about to walk into unknown danger. In that case, your intuition will let you know. But you have to really be present and attentive for you to hear it because it is gentle and quiet. The only way you can connect with your intuition is to be more aware. There are several ways for you to increase your awareness in this regard.

Moving your body is a great way to increase awareness and to hear your intuition more clearly. Intuition is simply communication from your higher self, angel guides, and spirit guides. This communication happens at the energy level, and movement helps with the flow of energy. So it follows that if you feel blocked and disconnected, you can move and release the old energy along your body. Any movement here serves the purpose. Whether it is from taking a walk, swimming, cooking, or working out. As long as there is a movement of energy, there will be a renewed connection with your higher self.

You can take note of your dreams and analyze them when you are awake. Often our intuition communicates important messages to us through our dreams. Still, we miss it because we don't put much thought into them.

Another great way to connect with your intuition is through journaling. This works best with a pen and paper. The best practice here is to write freely, with no thought and no filtering. Just put your pen on the paper and let the words fall out of you. Of course, sometimes, you may be so blocked that nothing comes out, and you spend hours just staring at a blank page. In such cases, you can give yourself a nudge by writing down a question or a statement that you think you need guidance on. Think of something that has been bothering you or that you are unsure of. It might take a while before something meaningful comes out from your pen, so a little patience is required for this exercise. Push through the jibber-jabber that may come out first and wait until you fall into a rhythm. You will be surprised at the insight you will gain once you start flowing.

Perhaps the most obvious way to connect with your intuition is to use. Intuition is like a muscle. The more you use it, the stronger it gets. People tend to ignore their intuition more than they realize because it's not loud. It can sometimes require you to do counterintuitive things. Your intuition comes like a silent whisper, a passing feeling, and so it's easy for it to get lost in a body that is filled with the loud distractions of this world. But the more you are present, the more precise the whisper becomes.

Similarly, because intuition is guidance from our spiritual self and may suggest counterintuitive things, we usually ignore it and rely on our intellect. But our intelligence is flawed and limited by what we know. In contrast, our intuition is informed by universal knowledge and wisdom.

Raise Energy through Your Chakras

According to various Hindu spiritual traditions, chakras are the cyclic energy centers that run along your spine and up to your head. Each one represents a different level of consciousness. Each chakra is represented by a different color and influences specific functions in the body. You can clear the energy blockage of a particular chakra through the use of crystals, infusions, physical exercises, and mantras associated with it. Alternatively, you can eat foods associated with the blocked chakra you wish to unlock.

The chakras can be powered by the Kundalini life force, which is dormant and lays coiled at the root chakra. Suppose you want to awaken the Kundalini life force at your root chakra. In that case, you will have to do Kundalini yoga which consists of meditation, breath work, and various poses meant to unlock the energy blockages at the location of your chakras. The life force can only be awakened when all seven chakras are open and aligned. Balancing a particular chakra allows you to channel the level of consciousness associated with it. Still, awakening the kundalini life force enables you to experience a spiritual awakening throughout all levels of consciousness. If one chakra is blocked, the life force cannot flow through all seven chakras.

The Seven Chakras

Your first chakra is the Root chakra, and it's located at the perineum and is red in color. It represents your sense of security and belonging and your ability to remain grounded in the physical world. The Root chakra controls your sex glands, your legs, kidneys, small intestine, and colon. When it is blocked, you will experience ailments such as poor circulation, infections in and around your sex glands, and constipation.

The Sacral chakra is second, and it's located in the genitals. It's orange and represents sexuality and your relationships with power, money, and your self-esteem. If you want to unlock the Root chakra, you can use the child's pose or the downward dancing dog pose and chant the LAM mantra. The Sacral chakra influences your spleen, uterus, large intestine, pelvis, and pancreas, to name a few. You will experience kidney and urinary tract infections, difficulty menstruating, and impotence when it is blocked. To unlock it, you can use the butterfly and cross-legged poses while chanting the VAM mantra.

The yellow Solar Plexus chakra, located at the navel and represents your sense of worth and value, is third. It influences your mood, adrenal glands, and your ability to digest food. You may experience indigestion, chronic fatigue, ulcers, and intense feelings of shame about your worth and self-respect when it is blocked. To unlock it, use the reverse plank and downward dog poses while chanting the RAM mantra.

The fourth chakra, known as the Heart chakra, is green and connects the three lower chakras to the three upper chakras. It represents unconditional love and is the ultimate source of light. This is the most important chakra for a lightworker because it is the source of their inner light and allows them to do their work with love and compassion. The heart chakra often becomes blocked when you hide your vulnerability and don't adequately express your feelings. This usually happens when we feel inundated with other people's energies or we experience a challenging time. When the heart chakra is blocked, you will experience chest pains. A deep disconnect with your higher self, fear, jealousy, heart issues, poor circulation, and experience feelings of apathy towards others. To unlock this chakra, use the bridge and fish poses while chanting the YAM mantra.

Fifth, we have the Throat chakra, the first of the upper chakras. It is blue in color and represents our ability to surrender to the universe and express its truths. When blocked, you struggle to express your feelings, you stutter often, and your throat is sore. If you want to activate this chakra, then you can chant the HAM mantra. You can also use fish and shoulder-stand poses.

We then have the sixth, indigo-colored Third Eye chakra, representing our connection to our intuition and abilities. If you are a Seer, then this chakra is your most powerful. It activates your clairvoyant skills and allows you to see multiple realities and perhaps even communicate with other souls telepathically. The Third Eye is located at the pineal gland, which secretes a hormone that regulates your circadian rhythm. So when it is blocked, you may experience insomnia, hypothyroidism or low blood pressure. The Third Eye chakra can be unlocked using the handstand and eagle poses, accompanied by the AUM mantra.

Lastly, we have the Crown chakra. It is violet or white in color and located at the top of your head. This seventh chakra is located at the pituitary gland. Because of this, it connects us to the universe by drawing its energy into our bodies. We come to realize its boundlessness. This chakra frees us from our limiting beliefs and views and allows us to experience a sense of pure bliss. When blocked, you can experience headaches, feel a complete lack of faith in the divine, and focus your awareness more on your mind and intellect.

Interestingly, because of the interconnected way in which the pituitary and pineal glands work with the hypothalamus. If the Crown chakra is blocked, so too is the Third Eye chakra and vice versa. If you want to unlock it, you can chant the OHM mantra while doing the lotus or saddle poses.

As mentioned above, there are various ways to unblock and raise energy through your chakras—the root of which is meditation. I will break down most of these separately, although they work together in any number of combinations.

Chakra Meditation

Mindfulness is the cornerstone of clearing and raising energy through your chakras. One of the simplest ways to do this is through chakra meditation. You can try the rainbow meditation, which uses the colors associated with each chakra as the object of your focus. You begin by sitting comfortably on a flat and sturdy surface, preferably cross-legged. Then, imagine a light the color associated with the chakra you want to unlock and feel the light as it warms the location of your chakra, slowly clearing it. Once the chakra has been opened, you can focus on moving the light energy up and onto the next chakra and changing color as it moves up. It's suggested that you begin at the Root chakra and work your way all the way up to the Crown chakra, thus unblocking and balancing all of them.

If you struggle to focus on the light energy, you can massage the area concerned with crystals and oils. This will increase the energy you are channeling, and the touch sensation will help draw your mind to the area.

Using Oils, Infusions, Gemstones, and Crystals to Raise Energy through Your Chakras

You can use essential oils, infusions, gemstones, or crystals to help you channel energy towards your chakra so you can open and balance it. The crystals increase the light energy you channel towards the blocked chakra, as they have their own energy frequencies. Furthermore, you can set healing intentions towards the crystal, and they will amplify them.

Here are some of the crystals, gemstones, oils, and infusions you can use to open and align your chakras:

- Root Chakra - onyx, red obsidian, ruby, ginger, and cypress
- Sacral Chakra - red jasper, amber, carnelian, jasmine, and sandalwood

- Solar Plexus Chakra - topaz, yellow amber, citrine, spearmint, and lemon
- Heart Chakra - moonstone, emerald, amazonite, rosewood, and eucalyptus
- Throat Chakra - sapphire, turquoise, frankincense, coriander, and peppermint
- Third Eye Chakra - lapis lazuli, amethyst, celestine, lemongrass, and orange
- Crown Chakra - quartz, amethyst, cedarwood, and ylang-ylang

Using Breath Work and Chanting to Raise Energy through Your Chakras

Yoga uses different breathing techniques to help you channel your energy towards a particular chakra. The combination of breath work and mantra chanting increases awareness between the body and mind, channeling your consciousness into the chakras.

To start, empty your lungs and sit in an upright, comfortable position. The key here is to take deep breaths through the nose and breathe out through the mouth. You will begin at the Root chakra, chanting the mantra associated with it (LAM) and feeling your voice's vibrations at the perineum. Continue like this as your work your way up to the Crown chakra. You can repeat this as many times as you feel necessary or until you can feel the energy flowing through your chakra.

Kundalini Yoga

If you want to balance and raise energy throughout all your chakras, then you can do Kundalini yoga. This type of yoga uses breath work, meditations, hand postures, yoga poses, and mantras to activate and uncoil the Kundalini life force situated at the Root chakra. When done correctly, you can feel the energy surge up across your body, and your consciousness rises, and your body strengthens.

One of the critical aspects of Kundalini yoga is the

different breathing techniques associated with each exercise. The most commonly used is known as the breath of fire. This technique is powered by the Solar Plexus chakra and utilizes deep, long, and rapid breaths. The navel is used as a pump to bring oxygen into the bloodstream while charging your body's electromagnetic field, which is centered in your Heart grid. It can be challenging to get used to this technique, but once your body gets used to the new breathing, it becomes easier to settle into its rhythm.

To start:

Find a comfortable position to sit in with a straightened back.

Release any tension from the body by relaxing your shoulders and your jaws.

Put your hands on your knees in the Gyan Mudra (the hand pose where the tips of your index finger and thumb are touching, but the rest of the fingers are stretched out).

Take a deep breath through your nose and into your lungs, expanding your stomach as you go.

Exhale by contracting your navel towards your spine.

Do this a few times and make sure that the inhales and exhales are of equal measure so that you can find the rhythm.

After some time, take a break and return to your normal breathing technique for a few seconds.

Repeat this cycle for as long as you feel comfortable, usually not more than 10 minutes at a time.

Breath of fire strengthens your navel and nervous system because it teaches you how to control your breathing. This is useful when you start hyperventilating in stressful situations.

When you combine the breath of fire (or any other breathing technique) with the various yoga poses and mantras, you have a set of exercises that can be used to unlock the chakras, known as kriyas. If you want to balance all your chakras, you can do any kriya that engages them simultaneously. For example, you can sit in the Easy Pose, which targets the Crown, Third Eye, Sacral, and Root chakras. You use either of your hands to lightly tap the area around your heart with gradually increasing and decreasing intensities, thus engaging the Heart chakra. Engage the Solar Plexus chakra by doing the breath of fire technique, and chant the HAM mantra to engage the Throat chakra.

Kundalini yoga is a very complex spiritual practice. All kriyas require patience and the guidance of a skilled yogi—especially if you are still new to the practice. If you want to use this method to balance your chakras, then it's best that you find a class to join with a certified teacher.

Find Stillness in Everyday Life

To find stillness in everyday life, you need to understand the inherent peace to be found in living, even amid chaos. The life of a lightworker can be emotionally exhausting, so it's important to learn how to focus on the silver lining amongst the clouds. You do this by intentionally creating a routine that allows you to periodically detach from the noise and be fully present in the pockets of peace that are present at any given moment.

For example, you can do this by starting your day with silent and mindful stretches right after you wake up. Feel as your body comes alive and the energy flows through it. You can then have a calming and hot shower and savor the feeling of warm water running over your body. In this moment of silence, you can think of all the things you are grateful for in your life. It can be anything at all. It doesn't matter how big or small it is. Practicing gratitude helps you to attract and manifest good things in your life. Next, you can sit down and set positive intentions for the day.

Another excellent way for you to find stillness is to have an item in your house, office, or on your body that reminds you of a moment when you were happy or feeling fulfilled. Train your mind to just take a moment to reminisce on that memory whenever your eyes land on that particular item. This is a simple yet highly effective way to learn how to take a moment to breathe and find a sense of calm throughout your day, especially when you feel overwhelmed with negativity.

You can set some time aside to read a book. This is a great way to ground yourself in the present because your mind is completely focused on the words you are reading. Your imagination is also fully engaged in building and bringing to life the words you are reading.

The moments of stillness don't have to be induced by anything. You can simply listen to the sounds around you at any given moment; observe the plants swaying to the wind. If you hear anything that distresses you, just let it pass by and don't have an emotional reaction to it. The important thing is to learn how to find peace even in the chaos. I find this habit particularly useful when you're having an especially bad day. There are days where you seem to be averting one crisis after another, and there is no moment of silence at all.

Sit into a Feeling of Joy-Bliss-Love-Light

The feeling of Joy-Bliss-Love-Light comes from the third and fourth chakras, which regulate your self-worth, willpower, and sense of unconditional love. To sit into this feeling, you need to focus your mind on the rhythm of your breathing in a meditative way. You can then slowly expand this focus on any other feeling that is present in your body. This is when you will feel what is known as the feeling of Joy-Bliss-Love-Light, which can be described as a warm, pulsating feeling. It is recommended that you do this every day because it makes you feel lighter the more you sit in it.

To fully explore this energy, you can chant the Sat Chit Ananda mantra. It is a compound Sanskrit word that describes the experience of Brahman, or ultimate reality, as it is conceptualized in Hindu philosophy. It represents the complete connectedness of all that is in existence. The mantra can also be translated as pure bliss consciousness, absolute bliss awareness, or actual bliss presence.

Sat represents the unchanging nature of the eternal. The pure truth lies at the center of all that is in nature, all that has an essence, and all that is in existence. It is the reality of everything. In the Upanishad (the Hindu religious texts), all perceivable through our mind, body, and spirit is pure truth. It is pure existence. But existence is not limited by what we can perceive. There is a plethora of worlds and beings that we are incapable of perceiving. In fact, our very understanding of Sat is limited by our minds and bodies because we can only process it as far as our physical beings can allow. When you are connected to your higher self, you gain a deeper understanding of your spirit's boundless and immortal nature and, by extension, of the infinitely unchanging universe.

Next, there is Chit, or the awareness/consciousness. It refers to a subjective presence and the things that your physical being allows you to focus on. Chit grants you the ability to experience reality through the senses. It's what makes it possible for you to comprehend the different scents in a garden, for example. This sensory awareness makes it possible for you to experience reality, albeit in a limited way as with Sat. But Chit goes beyond the thoughts and feelings we conceive in our minds—it transcends matter. Chit is what enables the body to function as it does and to experience existence. To be awakened is to comprehend Sat and Chit, that your being is boundless, that it has and will continue to consciously exist long after your physical body ceases to function.

Lastly, Ananda acknowledges bliss and joy as the natural state of being and an essential trait of universal energy. According to the Upanishad, total human happiness can be measured as such: A virile and youthful man of noble birth, well educated, and has access to all the wealth in the world. Such a man has no barriers preventing him from fulfilling any of his earthly desires, and he can fully feed his ego. It is through this medium that his sense of self is experienced. However, in other planes of existence, there is greater happiness to be found through better material objects, stronger bodies, and higher social ranks. And further still, there is an ascension of worlds in the universe, one offering more happiness than was conceivable in the previous world. So, if you are to chase happiness provided by objects and your senses, you will never be truly happy in this world.

However, suppose you can silence the noise and desires of this world and connect with your higher self. In that case, you will realize happiness itself is a mere reflection of the self. The nature of this self is bliss because the self desires nothing, having understood that the most authentic reality is that we are both nothing and everything. The higher self knows that nothing we have hoarded and defined ourselves by in the physical means anything because, in truth, we are all one. Once you stop allowing your sensory desires to rule you, you can better align with your higher self and achieve bliss. You realize that happiness is not something to be earned because it already is within you. Your higher self is boundless and neither dulled nor amplified by the medium through which you experience it. As such, the happiness that you could feel in the highest ascension level is the same as that to be felt through your human medium.

This is why enlightened beings don't preoccupy themselves with manufacturing and experiencing bliss. They understand that any medium that reflects the self already contains the highest level of happiness possible. So, even in moments we might deem as unpleasant, an enlightened being known that there is bliss to be found even in that.

At an instinctual level, this allows a child to be reunited with their best friend to experience the same amount of bliss as an adult who has just won the lottery. The sense of happiness is not created by the objects and subjects in question. Instead, it is a reflection of the bliss from within.

It's difficult to fully understand that bliss and joy come from within and not from the external. Primarily because our world focuses on creating happiness from material goods, feelings, and other external stimuli. But, the longer you sit in this feeling, the more you will come to understand and embrace it.

Become at Peace with Yourself and the World around You

An invaluable part of self-care as a lightworker is to become at peace with yourself and the world around you. Lightworkers are necessarily sensitive beings due to the nature of their calling, and they are constantly exposed to dark energy. Dark energy is like quicksand—the more you resist it, the faster it sucks you in. One of the best things a lightworker can learn is to accept this universal truth: The universe is a place of order, light, and bliss. While life on earth has an inherent peace, our planet is consumed by chaotic disorder and dark energy. It is easy for you to become consumed by this dark energy that overwhelms you and dims your light as a physical being.

Suppose you learn how to live in harmony and peace with others and maintain it regardless of the kind of external stimuli. In that case, you will remain in a state of joy even as you are surrounded by chaos. You need to learn how to master your emotions and live every moment with a sense of peace. As a sensitive to energies and exposed to a lot of different ones, learning to distinguish what is and isn't worth your energy is a vital skill. This doesn't mean that you need to ignore what is happening around you. That is unhealthy and unrealistic because you are required to be present at all times. If you consciously adopt a divine perspective on life, you can simply note the darkness and let it pass through your consciousness. In this way, you don't let the negative thoughts define you, and you don't obsess over them. Instead, you acknowledge and release them.

If you constantly obsess over these thoughts, you will end up manifesting them into your reality which makes you think about them more, and so the cycle continues. If you constantly talk negatively about yourself, you will miss the good things in your life and miss out on wonderful opportunities because you think you aren't worthy. This is why it's vital to master bringing your ego and shadow into harmony with each other. When you are in connection with your higher self, you experience moments where you glimpse your most authentic self. If you've seen your true self, you know that the negative self-image you have is not who you are. When you know who you are, no one can move you from that place of self-acceptance, not even your own mind.

Once you've come to a place of inner peace, you need to accept the world for what it is. It's dark and heavy on the soul. Society is driven by the need for perfection, and most people live their lives ruled by fear, anger, hate, and sadness. Humanity chases material gain because we think it will bring happiness, but the chase never ends. As soon as you have something, you want the next best thing. Suppose you can interact with everyone with love and from a place of understanding and compassion. In that case, you won't be riled up by every little negative thing. So, when people try to belittle your sense of self or project their insecurities onto you, you can just let that slide off you like water off a duck's back.

SEVEN

Meditation as a Lightworker

"THERE ARE TWO KINDS OF LIGHT—THE GLOW THAT ILLUMINATES, and the glare that obscures." -James Thurber

Over the past few years, meditation has become one the most commonly used methods to calm the mind and bring about a state of mind-body awareness. Generally, meditation increases awareness by training the mind to focus on a particular thing, a thought, or an object. This minimizes random thoughts passing through your mind, and if one should slip in there, you are taught how to control your reaction to it.

Our world is one of chaos and constant distractions. When your mind is filled with intrusive and chaotic thoughts, you tend to feel overwhelmed and completely distracted. When you meditate, you learn how to calmly acknowledge these thoughts and let them pass through your mind so that you can go back to focusing on your desired thought or object. This calm awareness helps connect you to your higher self because it releases dark energies and brings the mind and the body into unison. Meditation increases your concentration levels and reduces stress, pain, and anxiety. When practiced frequently, it can keep you mentally sharp for longer, reduce the habit of intense emotional reactivity, and increase your general levels of peace and contentment. There are various methods of meditation that you can use, and I will name a few below.

Body Scan Meditation

One of the easiest methods is called body scan meditation. You begin by taking deep, slow breaths and releasing any tension in your body by relaxing your jaws, shoulders, and all your joints. You can then channel your concentration to any particular body part, such as the feet, for example. Focus your mind on each step you take. Take note of which muscles pull and contract as you take your steps while still taking deep and deliberate breaths.

Once you have settled into this awareness, you can move your focus up to your knees. Past your pelvis, and into your core, through your fingertips, and up your back until you reach the top of your head. As you do this, you may feel energy gently pulsating through your body in the places where you are currently placing your attention.

You can repeat this as many times as you would like, always making sure to listen to your body if it wants you to stop.

Transcendental Meditation

You can also try transcendental meditation, which uses a specific phrase as the object of your attention. Usually, you can repeat a positive phrase, such as any of the following:

- *"I am loved and worthy."*
- *"I am capable."*
- *"I attract peace and joy."*
- *"I radiate love and happiness."*

You can also use any other phrase that you feel resonates with your soul. Using a positive phrase as your mantra helps focus your mind, attracts light energy into your being, and helps to dissolve negative self-talk.

Guided Imagery Meditation

You can try guided imagery, which uses the mind's eye to invoke positive and calming imagery as a stress and pain relief method. This usually requires you to be guided by someone else, but you can use recorded audio if you are alone.

During guided imagery, the practitioner uses deep breathing techniques to guide the patient into a relaxed and peaceful state. You, as the patient, are guided into creating imagery from your imagination, memory, or dreams that induce feelings of joy, peace, and happiness. This technique utilizes some or all of the senses. The practitioner may use candles, incense, or music to facilitate the imagery.

Guided imagery helps the patient connect to their intuition and creates a tranquil state that drives negative thoughts and emotions. The patient's peaceful state increases their capacity to absorb the light energy being channeled into them by the lightworker. It also promotes creativity, problem-solving, and awareness.

Resting Meditation

There is also what is known as resting meditation. This technique requires you to simply relax your mind. Don't think about anything, focus on anything, or listen to anything. This is harder than it sounds because our minds always have something going on for most of us, even when we are asleep.

Don't worry if you don't get this right at first. It takes time to master. Just let any thoughts that come to you pass by and continue your state of rest.

Transmute Your Own Shadows

In our previous discussion on shadow work, I mentioned that even as an awakened spiritual being, you still need to contend with your ego and your shadow. You do not achieve a complete unification of the soul until you have reached the final level of ascension, which is enlightenment. A lightworker is constantly interacting with the dark energy in others, and this can affect your energy field. If you don't clear this unwanted energy, it lowers your consciousness and leaves you feeling drained and overwhelmed. This reduced state of awareness strengthens your shadow because it feeds on low vibrational energies. This causes your ego to control your awareness, closing the connection to your higher self and the universe. When this happens, the best way to regain the connection is to bring your shadow into the conscious, thus transmuting the darkness. So, how do you transmute this shadow?

A lightworker's shadow is often triggered by people's energies or situations they encounter as they do their light work. Fortunately, you have experience transmuting your shadow, so the process should be familiar and more accessible for you now. When you feel your shadow trying to fill your energy field with dark energy, you need to take a moment and analyze what is happening. It's essential to take note of the triggers that present themselves as you interact with others. What characteristics tend to annoy you about people? Which behaviors are you prone to judging the harshest? You need to examine how you react to others and question why that is. Asking these questions will lead you to uncover past experiences where you or someone you know displayed similar characteristics or behaved in ways similar to those you now dislike, and you were shamed and shunned for it. These experiences make us repress vital parts of our being out of fear of being ostracized. That is how our egos try to protect us.

Now, whenever you see someone else do the thing you were not allowed to do or display characteristics that you were not allowed to explore, you react poorly. This could be because you are projecting your fear onto them, manifesting anger or judgment. It could also be that you came to believe that certain behaviors are an acceptable social response in that situation. Subsequently, you are mimicking the learned behavior. Whatever the case may be, you need to be honest with yourself and uncover the root of the matter. Once you've done this, you need to figure out what needs healing and what needs to simply be acknowledged and discarded.

Once you confront your shadow and embrace those parts of your soul that have been repressed and ignored, you transmute your shadow into light and consciousness. By constantly and intentionally embracing all of your thoughts and desires, you live an authentic life that helps you remain in alignment with your higher self.

Some people struggle to do all this inner work by themselves and may need the help of additional tools and resources. This is perfectly normal and nothing to be ashamed of. You are not a sham or a lesser lightworker for needing help with your healing. In fact, many people find that the best way to proceed along the journey of spiritual awakening is to combine the use of spiritual practices with tools, such as therapy. If you are struggling, ask the universe to bring you the right people to help you along your path.

As you can see, there are a lot of recurring themes under the different subheadings of self-care, such as movement, meditating, and connecting with nature. This should come as no surprise considering the interconnected nature of the universe and all that exists within it. Nothing is too minuscule or insignificant to obey the laws of the universe. Even something as personal as self-care falls perfectly into the order of the universe. The most important part of self-care is being honest to yourself about what you are feeling and being fully present in those feelings. When you learn how to authentically embrace all of who you are, your connection to your higher self strengthens. You can better discern what you need to do with every thought, feeling, and energy that comes your way. Your intuition, your guides, and the universe will all help you figure it out.

All of this takes time and practice. And even then, you may still experience an extremely bad day once in a while and struggle with your self-care.

EIGHT

Lightworker Syndrome

"What is soul? It's like electricity — we don't really know what it is, but it's a force that can light a room." -Ray Charles

During their spiritual awakening, lightworkers often experience periods where they have difficulty balancing their ego-mind perceptions of reality with their newfound higher consciousness. This can cause extreme uncertainty over how to successfully navigate this duality. As a result, many lightworkers feel sad, scared, and other dark emotions that radiate low energies. It then becomes difficult for the lightworker to continually vibrate higher while feeling like they may not live out your purpose.

Barbara Rogoski explains what she terms "the steps to the lightworker syndrome" that many lightworkers may experience once they begin raising their consciousness. According to Rogoski, lightworkers feel an overwhelming sense of excitement and relief in the early stages of their spiritual awakening. After a lifetime of troubles and feeling rudderless, they are finally experiencing a true sense of hope. Naturally, they will want to start doing impactful work as soon as possible. They wait for further guidance from the universe on how to start living their lives from a higher perspective.

After some time, impatience will start to rear its head if things are not progressing in the way they thought they would. They become restless at the perceived lack of direction and guidance. The initial euphoric high slowly becomes replaced with small pockets of self-doubt and confusion. To combat this, lightworkers start to actively seek out advice from the universe through the teachings and experiences of other lightworkers and enlightened masters. The problem with this is that the instructions of others are meant to guide you, not to direct you. New lightworkers often confuse these two things and may begin to follow someone else's life journey. This won't work, and their sense of confusion and stagnancy will continue.

Soon, impatience seeps in, and their frustration rises. Their newfound sense of love and purpose begins to feel like a burdening weight rather than a liberation. At this point, their limiting beliefs and the lightworkers start questioning the practicality and possibility of living an abundant and purpose-filled life. Their ego-mind starts worrying about how they will meet their physical needs while chasing this spiritual purpose. Understandably, they begin to feel angry at the universe for placing what seems to be an unattainable vision of their lives in their heart. Then not providing them with any directions on how they can practically live this life on Earth.

This is when they enter the complaints stage. Their panic and frustration manifest in constant complaints to their friends and family on the universe's perceived unresponsiveness. This is when depressive moods set in. The lightworkers feel like giving up on pursuing a better, higher lifestyle and returning to the comfort of life as they knew it. Firmly rooted in the limitations of the ego-mind and their physical reality.

Rogoski advises newly awakened lightworkers to "release the urge to serve" and trust in the predestined timing of their spiritual journey. Instead of letting their frustrations and fears vex them, they can use this transitional period as an opportunity to mentally prepare for the lifestyle shift necessary to live at a higher perspective.

This is what lightworker syndrome looks like. You struggle with various dark energy emotions as you stress over how you will feed yourself and pay for your bills while living a purpose-driven life. These emotions make it difficult for you to stay connected to your higher self. Instead of manifesting light and love, your energy field is blocked by low vibrational frequencies.

Spiritual Connectedness vs. Physical Groundedness

When you are experiencing lightworker syndrome, you feel like you can't balance your heightened state of consciousness and fulfill your purpose with financially fruitful work. You get drawn into an either-or mentality, where you think you can either do work that has sound financial benefits but is not aligned with your purpose and leaves you disappointed or do work that is spiritually rewarding but leaves you unable to sufficiently provide for yourself and your family. You believe that you can't be spiritually connected and physically grounded at the same time. This kind of thinking leaves you in a whirl of despair because you cannot work efficiently and make good money while feeling disconnected from Source. This state of affairs naturally leaves you feeling melancholic and blocks your energy because you draw on low energies.

While this is a valid concern, the fatal misconception held by lightworkers is that there needs to be a sacrifice. They cannot do work aligned with their purpose while simultaneously attaining financial security. This fear is often experienced by lightworkers who are called to do not mainstream or conventional work in what they think is an oversaturated market or field. They forget that the spirit operates on the principles of order and unity. Your existence on this planet is evidence that there is a need for your voice and your work.

The universe wants to and will help you gravitate towards paths that provide a sustainable way to bring your spiritual and physical needs into harmony.

When you feel connected to the Source and stay true to your higher self, you become flooded with light energy, bringing peace and tranquility. Leaving you energized for the work you need to do here on Earth. This then feeds into your work, allowing you to do more with your time, make more money, and possibly reach more people.

Fearing Your Own Power

One of the reasons you may struggle with the idea of balancing spiritual connectedness and physical groundedness as a new lightworker is that you subconsciously fear your own power. Change is difficult for any person because our brains are wired to fear the unknown. It follows that there may be some resistance from your ego-self as you begin to completely let go of your old identity and fully step into your higher self.

When you raise your consciousness, you open new energy fields, enabling you to do things you previously thought impossible. Whether you know it or not, the limiting beliefs you had may still be making you believe that you cannot have it all. Your ego-mind can only perceive what is visible in the physical world. It is crafted to protect you from being hurt or disappointed. When you look around, all you see is scarcity and competition for resources.

On the other hand, your higher self tells you that there is abundance and fulfillment in your purpose, far beyond what you can see. It's only natural that when you try to live your life according to this unseen abundance, your ego-mind will try to protect you. It knows that you are moving towards uncharted waters, based on the understanding not supported by the senses.

This is one of those instances where you need to bring

your ego in harmony with your soul. When you try to ascend to the next spiritual level, your deepest fears and insecurities will come to the fore and wrestle with you. The concerns over whether you are enough or have enough manifest themselves in fear, anxiety, and confusion. These causes distrust and disconnect between your inner self (the ego's physical being controlled) and your higher self. While it does become easier to silence your ego as you vibrate more elevated, the truth is that until you achieve enlightenment, you still operate as though there is a division between you and everything else. Your success as a lightworker relies on you leaning fully into your higher self and trust in the divine timing of the universe.

Once you realize that despite what your ego-mind tells you, there is an abundance in the universe that transcends your senses and is accessible to you. You will realize that there is no need to think that you must sacrifice either your purpose or physical needs. When you are connected to your higher self and doing work that fulfills your goal (and thereby fulfills you), you are at peace. You are not fatigued by the fear and anxiety that comes with worrying about having enough of life's necessities. This allows you to work more and reach more people, which mean you earn more. Nothing good comes with fearing your power, and your purpose won't go away simply because you are afraid to step into it.

What Happens if You Succeed?

Your limiting beliefs also make you fear your success. You don't know what it looks like to live a life of financial abundance and spiritual prosperity. So you unconsciously shy away from this unknown. But what will happen if you resonate with your purpose and fully step into your power? Success—that's what will happen!

Steve Pavlina writes that fearing your own power is actually a fear of the responsibility that comes with that power. As a lightworker, your work is meant to benefit mankind and help raise the collective consciousness. The more people you help, the greater your responsibility is. Understandably, you may find this realization daunting, but trust that you will overcome this fear. You need to understand that your higher self is an eternal, never-changing being and trust in the orderly intentionality of the universe. If you have the capacity for more responsibility, then you are capable of handling that responsibility. Your power determines your responsibility, and you don't escape it by not acting on it.

Any concerns or struggles you have with balancing your spiritual connectedness with your physical groundedness are just manifestations of your failure to accept your power. You can access that power in this dimension. Once you stop echoing your fears and limiting beliefs back to yourself, you will begin manifesting the abundance and success attached to your purpose in the physical world.

Conclusion

"Knowledge is wisdom's treasure." –*Anonymous*

While turning the pages of this book, you learned all about being a lightworker. You learned of their purpose in this world, of their need for self-realization before they can begin honoring their calling, and of the difficulties they face during their odyssey. You came to understand how dimensions of the universe work and how lightworkers interact with these at various times while bringing light to our planet. You were shown how to identify a lightworker by their personality and how you can take care of your health once you've decided to embark on the path to spiritual awakening. You were shown how lightworkers can balance the needs of their bodies with the nourishment of their souls. You now know that even with a plethora of well-paying jobs available to them, there will still be a fear of letting go of the old and stepping fully into a new way of life.

These pages are filled with knowledge on the spiritual and physical journeys of a lightworker. You are now privy to the joys and pitfalls of a lightworker's life. It's not easy to follow your calling as a lightworker in a world drowning in darkness and a body that limits your understanding of the universe. But it is fulfilling and infinitely more joyous than any life lived denying your most authentic self.

With all that you have learned, you can now make an informed decision on whether or not you want to take up the mantle of light working in servitude to the spirit and the greater good of mankind. Remember that knowledge is useless if you don't use it to effect a change in your life. If you are indeed a lightworker, then the effects of life will reverberate throughout history long after your physical body has perished.

Maybe this was the wake-up call you needed to start the life you were destined for. You have the knowledge. You have the tools. The question now is: What are you going to do with it?

References

Ascension. (2013, October 3). *The difference between spirit, soul and ego.* http://www.ascension.bg/en/ascension-en/ascension-more/340-soul-spirit-eng

Ash. (2019, December 13). *How to move energy through your chakras | high vibes haven.* Highvibeshaven.com. https://highvibeshaven.com/how-to-move-energy-up-your-chakras/

Asking Angels. (n.d.). *Lightworker jobs and work, what can light-bearers do?* http://askingangels.com/articles/spiritual/lightworker-jobs.php

Beckler, M. (2017, May 11). *The 11 types of lightworkers - Which one are you?* Gostica. https://gostica.com/spiritual-growth/11-types-lightworkers/

Blavatsky Theosophy. (2019, April 15). *The difference between soul and spirit.* https://blavatskytheosophy.com/the-difference-between-soul-and-spirit/

Colvin, A. P. (2021, January 17). *Guided imagery and visualization*

References

meditation what's the difference? Amy Pattee Colvin. https://www.amypatteecolvin.com/guided-imagery-and-visualization-meditation/

Destination Deluxe. (2020, May 29). *Sacred geometry explained - What is the meaning behind the patterns?* https://destinationdeluxe.com/sacred-geometry-explained-healing-benefits/#:~:text=Sacred%20 geometry%20is%20considered%20an%20ancient%20 science%20that

Ford, T. (2019, January 20). *Kriya - For the heart chakra.* Shakta Kaur. https://www.shaktakaur.com/post/kriya-for-the-heart-chakra#:~:text=Kriya%20-%20For%20the%20-Heart%20Chakra%20Sit%20in

Fosu, K. (2020, November 24). *Shadow work: A simple guide to transcending the darker aspects of yourself.* Big Self Society. https://medium.com/big-self-society/shadow-work-a-simple-guide-to-transcending-the-darker-aspects-of-the-self-e948ee285723

Gaia. (2020, December 3). *Akashic records 101: What are they and how to access them.* https://www.gaia.com/article/akashic-records-101-can-we-access-our-akashic-records

Gawain, S. (2011). *Living in the light: Follow your inner guidance to create a new life and a new world.* New World Library.

Hogan, B. (2021, April 5). *What is a lightworker? Learn all about these "illuminated" humans.* Scary Mommy. https://www.scarymommy.com/lightworker/

Hoy, T. (2014, June 20). *Gut feeling: Psychic messages from your guides and angels by Tana Hoy.*

References

Tana Hoy. https://www.tanahoy.com/gut-feeling/

In My Sacred Space. (2015, August 20). *Understanding dimensions, densities and ascension.* https://inmysacredspace.com/understanding-dimensions-densities-and-ascension/

King, S. (2018, March 23). *Earth's grids and portals: Gateways of light and unity.* healing energy tools. https://www.healingenergytools.com/earth-grids/

Larkin, B. (2021, April 7). *Chakra yoga: The best yoga poses to balance your 7 chakras.* Brett Larkin Yoga. https://www.brettlarkin.com/chakra-yoga-poses/

Lew, A. (2021, June 30). *Explainer: What are the different spiritual dimensions of reality?* Medium. https://medium.com/new-earth-consciousness/explainer-what-are-the-different-spiritual-dimensions-of-reality-and-is-earth-moving-to-the-5th-2cd99d3dc319

Miller, A. (n.d.). *How to do Kundalini breath of fire.* Healthy Living. https://healthyliving.azcentral.com/kundalini-breath-fire-8269.html

Ortega, A. (2020, April 3). *What is a lightworker - Discover if you are a lightworker too.* Manifestation Matters. https://manifestationmatters.com/what-is-a-lightworker-discover-if-you-are-a-lightworker-too/

Pavlina, S. (2006, November 13). *Lightworker syndrome – Steve Pavlina.* Stevepavlina.com. https://stevepavlina.com/blog/2006/11/lightworker-syndrome/

Petrylaite, G. (2018, November 16). *A beginner's guide on chakra alignment (with how to videos).* Change Your Energy.

References

https://www.changeyourenergy.com/blog/672/a-beginners-guide-on-chakra-alignment

Psychic Source. (2021, May 11). *Are you a lightworker? | quiz | psychic source.* https://www.psychicsource.com/article/life-destiny-meaning/are-you-a-lightworker-quiz-psychic-source/18901#

Rogoski, B. (2009, November 6). *The lightworkers' syndrome.* EzineArticles. https://ezinearticles.com/?The-Lightworkers-Syndrome&id=3207715

Salow, S. (2015). *Find yourself: Go the distance to discover your meaning.* Self published.

Scott. (2021, May 1). *What are the different Tai Chi styles and which Should I study?* Tai Chi Basics. https://taichibasics.com/tai-chi-styles/

Shah, S., & Merrill, D. (2020, June 12). *The 5 most common types of meditation — And how to choose the best type for you.* Business Insider Australia. https://www.businessinsider.com.au/types-of-meditation-2020-6

Sol, M. (2018, February 26). *5 different forms of spiritual ascension - Which have you experienced?* LonerWolf. https://lonerwolf.com/spiritual-ascension/

Spirituality. (2019, December 6). *There are 12 types of lightworkers! What kind of lightworker are you?* https://blog.spiritualify.com/there-are-12-types-of-lightworkers-what-kind-of-lightworker-are-you/

The Joy Within. (2019a, May 19). *Satcitananda mantra meditation*

References

- *Attaining pure bliss consciousness*. The Joy Within. https://thejoywithin.org/meditations/mantras/satcitananda

The Joy Within. (2019b, June 26). *How to activate your light body*. https://thejoywithin.org/spirituality/how-to-activate-your-light-body

The Tai Chi effect. (n.d.). *Main 5 styles of Tai Chi*. https://thetaichieffect.com/styles-of-tai-chi/

Vera. (2016, October 8). *3D, 4D and 5D – The Dimensions and their differences*. Wake up Experience. https://thewakeupexperience.eu/3d-4d-and-5d-the-dimensions-and-their-differences/

Wiest, B. (2018, March 12). *20 Signs you're what's known as a "lightworker"*. Thought Catalog. https://thoughtcatalog.com/brianna-wiest/2018/03/20-signs-youre-whats-known-as-a-lightworker/

About the Author

Monique Joiner Siedlak is a writer, witch, and warrior on a mission to awaken people to their greatest potential through the power of storytelling infused with mysticism, modern paganism, and new age spirituality. At the young age of 12, she began rigorously studying the fascinating philosophy of Wicca. By the time she was 20, she was self-initiated into the craft, and hasn't looked back ever since. To this day, she has authored over 50 books pertaining to the magick and mysteries of life.

To find out more about Monique Joiner Siedlak artistically, spiritually, and personally, feel free to visit her **official website**.

www.mojosiedlak.com

facebook.com/mojosiedlak
twitter.com/mojosiedlak
instagram.com/mojosiedlak
pinterest.com/mojosiedlak
bookbub.com/authors/monique-joiner-siedlak

Other Books by the Author

African Spirituality Beliefs and Practices

Hoodoo

Seven African Powers: The Orishas

Cooking for the Orishas

Lucumi: The Ways of Santeria

Voodoo of Louisiana

Haitian Vodou

Orishas of Trinidad

Connecting With Your Ancestors

Black Magic

The Orishas

Vodun: West Africa's Spiritual Life

Marie Laveau: Life of a Voodoo Queen

Practical Magick

Wiccan Basics

Candle Magick

Wiccan Spells

Love Spells

Abundance Spells

Herb Magick

Moon Magick

Creating Your Own Spells

Gypsy Magic

Protection Magick

Celtic Magick

Divination Magic for Beginners

Divination with Runes: A Beginner's Guide to Rune Casting

Divination with Diloggún: A Beginner's Guide to Diloggún and Obi

Get a Handle on Life

Stress Management

Get a Handle on Anxiety

Get a Handle on Depression

Get a Handle on Procrastination

The Yoga Collective

Yoga for Beginners

Yoga for Stress

Yoga for Back Pain

Yoga for Weight Loss

Yoga for Flexibility

Yoga for Advanced Beginners

Yoga for Fitness

Yoga for Runners

Yoga for Energy

Yoga for Your Sex Life

Yoga to Beat Depression and Anxiety

Yoga for Menstruation

Yoga to Detox Your Body

Yoga to Tone Your Body

A Natural Beautiful You

Creating Your Own Body Butter

Creating Your Own Body Scrub

Creating Your Own Body Spray

Last Chance Join My Newsletter!

If you missed it, I have a free gift available for you and wanted to remind you it's still available.

mojosiedlak.com/self-help-and-yoga-newsletter

Thank you for reading my book.
I really appreciate all your feedback and would love to hear what you have to say! Please leave your review at your favorite retailer!

www.ingramcontent.com/pod-product-compliance
Lightning Source LLC
Chambersburg PA
CBHW071259040426
42444CB00009B/1782